FOREWORD

ANDREW LOOG OLDHAM

Peter Meaden gave me life and changed it and gave it a future. He made it better. He made it actual. I think he did the same for The Who.

In this game of life that we are all pawns in, somebody has to let you in, somebody has to open the door. In the late Sixties or Seventies, I sat on a beach in the Hamptons with the American movie actor Tony Curtis. We had bonded over the drugs we were both doing and our fond recollections of Mick and John, two London hashish dealers who had served me so well back in the day and had served Mr. Curtis whilst he resided on Chester Square in London filming *The Persuaders* TV series with ex-Saint, Roger Moore.

"Somebody has to let you in," Curtis informed me. We had both seen better times according to the rest of the world, but all seemed right with mine as we licked our wounds with cashmere on that Yankee beach. Curtis had one of the same abilities that Peter Meaden had. When he was on you, was hustling you, was plain and simply talking to you, you felt like you were the only person in his world. Meaden had that gift, that passion. Ask Daltrey, ask Pete...

"My mistake," the actor continued, "was that I shat on the man who let me it.... It was Lew Wasserman, Andy. He was my agent before he became the King of Hollywood. I got big and he wanted me to do the TV series *With Cockamamie*, I thought I was too big for TV. I said no. Wasserman never forgave me. He blackballed me for many, many years. That's how I ended doing all the crap I did to pay the rent. "

I never said no to Meaden. He said no to himself. In some ways he mirrored the rise and fall of Rolling Stones' founder, guitarist, Brian Jones. Youth sometimes shows no mercy as we lived in our rock 'n' roll *Lord of the Flies*-like times. On occasion, I let Peter embarrass me, as I did Brian Jones, which is ridiculous, and part of the stupidity of the time. Both gave so much, both were cats who had had nine lives, and somebody up there decided to send them back for a 10th. Peter and Brian both did their brilliance then got recalled. Brian a founder member of the 27 club – Peter the unique king of the 37 club.

Peter single handedly put The Who through school. Lambert and Stamp came later. Peter had already given them their reality imprint – he gave them mod. He gave them the sum parts of what he was, alas, not leaving enough for himself to survive on. This is not a knock on The Who, it's just actuality.

Peter was four years older than me, an important four years. Peter came from Edmonton N 18, or some barren turf, before all of London became unaffordable. I came from Hampstead NW 3 which always was.

Peter had a motorbike with a sidecar and a lively bird called Gina. She gave him life as he fueled mine. He took me into Soho and he took me to Ronan O'Rahilly's Scene club. He introduced me to American clobber.

At the time, 1960, Peter was on his way to mod. We could not afford Austin's, the small shop next door to Cecil Gee's on Shaftesbury Avenue. Cecil Gee was the equivalent of Versace meets D & G; Austin's was jazz meets Brioni. We could not afford that so Peter would take me to C & A's on Oxford Street near Marble Arch, where he would hustle the staff on the Men's floor as to when the occasional rack of unlined, three button, staggered-vent American suits (bottle-green preferred) would be arriving.

Peter helped me dress for life. He still does. I knew Peter on his rise and search for the magic kingdom; the rest of that is yours, I'm more than happy with mine.

Andrew Loog Oldham managed The Rolling Stones (1963-1967) and founded Immediate Records (1965-1970). He is the author of Stoned, 2Stoned *and* Rolling Stoned.

8

King Mob

This edition © Red Planet Books 2024
Text © Steve Turner 2024
Cover design by Phillip Savill

ISBN: 978 1 9127 3351 4

Printed and bound by CPI Group (UK) Ltd, Croydon CR0 4YY

www.redplanetmusicbooks.com
email: info@redplanetbooks.co.uk

"Mod meant a hell of a lot to Pete Meaden. It meant a hell of a lot to me too, but I think it meant more to him than anybody else in the world. He was King Mod."

Pete Townshend, in conversation
with the author

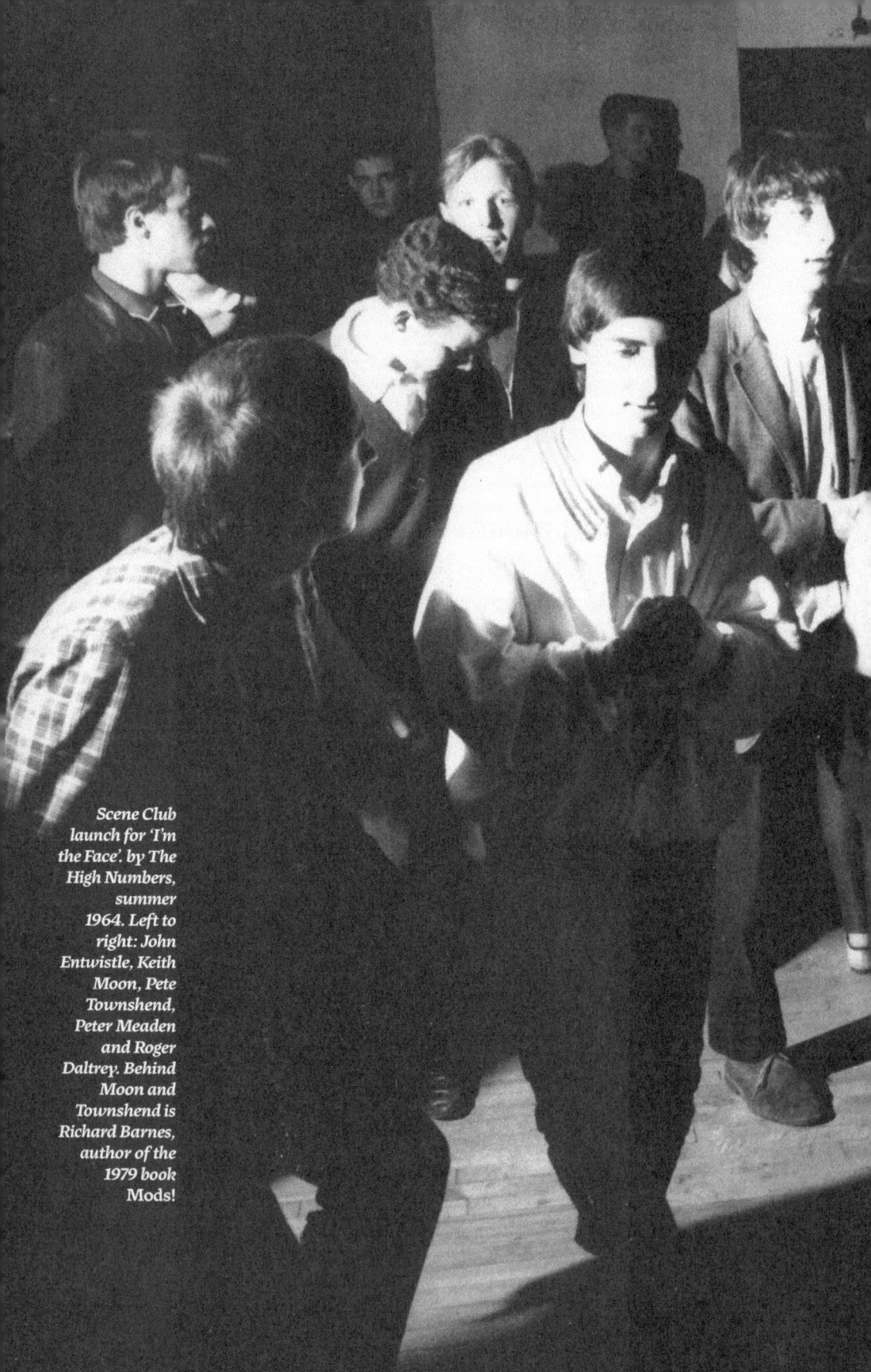

Scene Club launch for 'I'm the Face'. by The High Numbers, summer 1964. Left to right: John Entwistle, Keith Moon, Pete Townshend, Peter Meaden and Roger Daltrey. Behind Moon and Townshend is Richard Barnes, author of the 1979 book Mods!

"He was King, well he was King Mod, that was for sure. He was plugged into everything and lived a word, a sentence, a style, a dance, a step, ahead of everyone else."

'Irish Jack' Lyons, original Shepherd's Bush mod

"I am the mod who made mods out of The Who. I made The Who into mods."

Peter Meaden, in conversation with the author

BIOGRAPHY

Like Rolling Stones' manager Andrew Loog Oldham and guitarist Eric Clapton, Peter Meaden was the product of a wartime romance between an English woman and a North American serviceman stationed in Europe. Rosina Florence Alexander, a teacher employed by a school in Guildford, had met her temporary beau, a Canadian airman, in London in 1940, probably at a dance hall, and she'd fallen pregnant. She was already dating Stanley William Wayson Meaden, a 34-year old furniture polisher then serving as a driver in the Royal Army Ordnance Corps. A quiet and mild man, Stanley decided to spare her any possible future shame by marrying her when he was home on leave and the couple later set up home at 78 Palmerston Crescent in Palmers Green, North London.

Peter Alexander Edwin Meaden (Alexander after his mother's maiden name, Edwin after his father's brother) was born on Armistice Day 1941. His genetic father's name was not put on the birth certificate. Three years later a brother, Gerald, was born. Nothing was ever said about Peter's father and he naturally grew up believing he was descended from Stanley. He didn't find out the true story until he was in his thirties when the discovery both excited and disturbed him.

He attended the local Church of England primary school, St Michael's Palmers Green, and then went to Enfield Grammar School after passing his 11+ examination in 1952. Two years later the furniture company Courts offered Stanley a job in Farnham, Surrey, with a spacious five-bedroom company flat on Tilford Road close to the station. Stanley grabbed the opportunity of a secure job with a larger home outside London and after relocating Peter joined the third form of Farnham Grammar School in September 1954.

Peter Meaden and school didn't get on well. His reports read like those of John Lennon, another artistic boy whose

Opposite: Peter Meaden and his younger brother Gerald on Trafalgar Square, around 1950. Both boys proudly wearing the school caps and scarves of St. Michael's, Palmers Green

intelligence wasn't suited to formal education. He never got A grades, rarely got B grades and got only a modest C in the majority of subjects. He was best at English and art and worst at music and algebra. By the time he approached his GCEs, teachers were complaining of his "slack attitude" and saying that he was "capable of much more effort." By the time of his final year even his English master was stating that it was "a pity he needs so much prodding." His French teacher commented; "Has ability, but his attitude is so silly at times."

In the third and fourth forms he behaved himself but by the end of the spring term of the fifth form he had already been given three detentions. "The overall picture," summarised his form master Mr. Foster, "is of a capable boy who is throwing away his chances by lack of effort in the subjects which do not interest him."

The subjects that held his interest were history, English and art – subjects that would serve him well in the future. He was already reading a lot for pleasure and was fascinated with all things American. His brother Gerald also remembers him developing a passion for Nazi memorabilia, not out of an interest in Nazi ideology but because he admired the style of the badges and uniforms (some of which were designed by Hugo Boss). "He had German helmets, swastikas, armbands and things like that in his room," he recalls. "It was just a bit of anti-establishment fun. Everything he did was anti stuffy middle-class public school."

Family dynamics played a big part in shaping his character. Although she spared herself the indignity of being an unwed mother Rosina never overcame the feeling that she had married beneath her status. Her sister Elsie had become a fashion designer and was already travelling to Paris in the Thirties for the couture shows. Another sister, May, married an army officer and moved to India. Their daughter, who after marriage became Joyce Cuming, studied at the Slade School of Fine Art

Opposite: Peter's school report from 1957 – 'a capable lad throwing away his chances by lack of effort'

FARNHAM GRAMMAR SCHOOL

REPORT FOR *Spring* TERM, 19 57

NAME *Meaden P.A.* FORM *IV*

AD. 1578

AGE *15·4* AVERAGE AGE *15·2*

HALF-DAYS ABSENT — DETENTIONS *3*

Subject	Set	Mark	%	Av.	Posn.	
English	U	C	50	56	22/36	A pity he needs so much prodding as he is quite capable. He should realise he is the loser if he allows his attention to wander.
English Literature						
History						
Geography		C+	45	34	7/31	With a little more drive he could be very good. Written work could be more precise.
French	L	C	49	40	8/29	Has ability — but his attitude is so silly at times.
Latin						
Chemistry	L	C+	59	31	1/29	A Good Effort.
Physics	L	C+	53	31	1/35	Has ability.
Arithmetic			54	44	8/28	Algebra a weak spot, but he is trying hard.
Algebra	L	D	12	36	24/27	
Geometry			37	43	15/28	
Art		B+	70	50	3/32	Seems to be coming round to the idea of making the most of his undoubted ability. Keep it up.
Music						
Manual Instruction						
Physical Education		C				

Out of School activities

C.C.F. recruit

House Master

There are a few signs of improvement here, but the overall picture is of a capable boy who is throwing away his chances by lack of effort in those subjects which do not interest him. Let us see more comments like those on the Science subjects next term. These detentions are three too many.

M. C. Foster Form Master

and was a leading botanical artist. Rosina, who was a teacher at Weybourn School in Guildford in 1939, seemed destined to live a more prosaic life.

Although kindly, hardworking and honourable, Stanley Meaden lacked dynamism. He was neither a go-getter nor a man of the world. Perhaps for this reason Rosina placed a lot of her hopes in her eldest son. She wanted him to succeed where she had failed and didn't want him to become another version of the man she had married. As a later psychiatric report on Peter would put it: "The family atmosphere was always felt by Peter to be very insecure both emotionally and materially. His mother came from a middle-class background and he felt that she was overprotective and had rather high expectations for him. His step-father came from a working-class background."

For his part, Peter didn't want to turn into a junior version of the man he knew as Dad. He found his existence stifling and repetitious. There was nothing on Meaden Sr.'s horizon other than more polishing. It was a similar background to the ones that had prompted the rise of the so-called Angry Young Men generation of writers. John Osborne, who would write the groundbreaking play *Look Back in Anger* (1956), remembered his childhood home in Stoneleigh, Surrey, as "a terminus of semi-detached inertia." Of his family Osborne commented; "Spontaneity was bad breath to them."

Music wasn't a major force in Peter's life in the Fifties. He liked Elvis and Chuck Berry, but no more than any other teenager of the time. He also liked Gene Vincent, but his friends suspected it was more for Vincent's leather jacket and jeans than for his sound. In 1957 his style bias was more in the direction of the rockers than the fledgling modernists who raved about Miles Davis and favoured tailored suits. Like Arthur Seaton, the protagonist in Alan Sillitoe's 1958 novel *Saturday Night, Sunday Morning*, entertainment was more of a relief from the daily boredom and low expectations of post-war Britain than the

*Opposite:
One of Peter's
early musical
heroes was
Gene Vincent,
but perhaps
more for his
leather jackets
than his records*

heart of a new way of life.

He briefly considered a career as a salesman with Olivetti typewriters who were targeting Grammar School boys leaving school straight after GCE O levels but instead, in September 1957, joined Farnham College of Art to embark on a two-year Intermediate Certificate in Art and Crafts.

Following the war, the government had been alarmed that British art and design was lagging behind that of America and Europe and set up a committee to research ways in which Britain could become competitive in these prestigious areas of culture. As a result of this new art schools and colleges were established along with a four-year programme of study that would eventually earn students the newly created National Diploma in Design.

These educational changes were foundational to the Sixties explosion in youthful creativity. A new generation of young people like Peter with little appetite for formality, routine and conventional learning were given fresh opportunity to excel by using their imaginations. It produced artists like David Hockney and Peter Blake (Royal College of Art), rock musicians like John Lennon (Liverpool), Keith Richards (Sidcup) and Pete Townshend (Ealing), designers like Terence Conran (Central), Ossie Clark (Manchester) and Mary Quant (Goldsmiths), multi-talented eccentrics like Vivian Stanshall (Walthamstow) and photographers like Brian Duffy (St Martins) and Clive Arrowsmith (Kingston). Although not everyone went on to pursue the craft they majored in – graphic designers became lead guitarists, illustrators became copywriters, sculptors became light show designers – they all benefited from their enriched understanding of the creative process and the pop musician knew a lot about film and posters and the publicist knew about typefaces and portrait photography.

During his course at Farnham Peter was given a broad foundation. He was trained in figure drawing, modelling, still

Opposite:
First passport
photograph,
June 1959,
when Peter
was 17

life and pictorial composition and had the opportunity to pursue lithography and lettering. The emphasis all along was on the realistic portrayal of reality. It wasn't the time for abstraction or experimentation.

In 1958 he had two run-ins with the police. The first came when he tried to sell a gun he'd acquired (according to Gerald he found the weapon on Frensham Common in Surrey, an area used for military training during the war). Unfortunately, the person he approached was a plain-clothed member of the Flying Squad. Then he was arrested for stealing a car for joy riding. He was put on probation. Stanley and Rosina were beside themselves with worry. At a time of national concern over Teddy boys and juvenile delinquency their own son was turning into a teenage monster.

After Farnham he went to Guildford School of Art with the intention of doing a further two years in order to get his National Diploma in Design. During this time he met the future inventor Iain Sinclair, two years his junior, who would later provide him his entré to fashionable Hampstead society. They came across each other in 1959 at Guildford's first coffee shop, an upstairs room near Tunsgate Arch (124 High Street) called Boxers, and Sinclair became one of the few people to witness Peter Meaden at close quarters during his transition from small town art student to London scene maker.

Peter was increasingly frustrated by the constraints of his background. There was nothing in the lifestyle of his parents that he aspired to. He found them small-minded, unadventurous and colourless. He wanted to live in the fast lane and had already been inspired by Jack Kerouac's novel *On the Road*. "He didn't feel Mum and Dad had any ambition," remembers his brother Gerald. "Dad wasn't earning a lot of money as a French polisher and Peter was a bit contemptuous of that."

In Iain he saw someone from a much more privileged background who had a good mind and was determined to use it.

Opposite: Inventor and designer Iain Sinclair, pictured in 1961. He introduced Peter to Hampstead society while Peter introduced him to fashion, style, James Bond, and Mickey Spillane

Iain's father and grandfather had both been successful engineers and his older brother, the soon-to-be-famous inventor Clive Sinclair, was already designing and selling radio components and had authored his first book at the age of 18. At the same time Iain saw in Peter someone who was slightly older than him and who could educate him in the ways of the world.

"I'd always been interested in clothes, but he knew a lot more about clothes and styling than I did. I think he might have spotted that he was on a higher level than I was in that respect. I knew I had a lot to learn in that respect and he was the right sort of bloke to know. He always read a lot. He introduced me to James Bond. He'd spotted him when he was serialised in the *Daily Express*, long before the films came out. And he liked Mickey Spillane. I would never have heard of these people if it hadn't been for Peter. He loved Mickey Spillane."

In late 1959 or 1960 Iain's family moved from Guildford to Hampstead in North London where they had a top floor flat in a mansion block just off the High Street. The dancer Margot Fonteyn, then working for the Royal Ballet, lived on the opposite side of the road. His new friends were the sons and daughters of the wealthy and intellectual elite who were experimenting with bohemianism. There were plenty of coffee bars, restaurants and wine bars, the Everyman specialised in showing 'continental' films and there was folk music at the Witches Cauldron in Belsize Lane.

Opposite: Peter first discovered James Bond through John McLusky's 1958 strip cartoon in the Daily Express. *He admired Bond's sense of adventure and his attention to style and detail*

Peter, who found Farnham and Guildford too provincial, saw the new Sinclair home as a free place to stay at weekends and an escape from his lower middle-class environment. He loved the ambience of Hampstead and Belsize Park – the huge houses, the wealthy inhabitants, the intellectual buzz that came from it being a haven for artists, authors, and politicians and the free-and-easy lifestyles of the young nouveau riche.

Susie Orbach, now known as a therapist, author and social critic, was part of the crowd he mixed with. Her mother was

a New Yorker and her father was a Labour politician who'd recently lost his seat in Willesden. "Like many young people we were trying to find our identity," she says. "The local bohemian-jazz-drug-left-politico scenes all folded into one. We hung out at The Cruel Sea pub that was on Heath Street and at what is now The Forum in Kentish Town. We tried to be ever-so grown up by reading Sunday newspapers over 'brunch' and listening to jazz."

"Peter wanted to move to London," says Sinclair. "He was fed up with Farnham. So, he became a sort of 'unwelcome guest' at our flat. He just sort of came and camped without permission. I remember him looking around various places to find a room to rent but not being able to find anything."

Then, in 1960, Stanley Meaden's father, Frederick, who was still renting in Cuthbert Road, Edmonton, fell ill and the landlord judged that he needed live-in care so the Meaden family moved back to London to look after him. He died soon after his family arrived and so Stanley took over the rental. Having tasted the privileged life of Hampstead, Peter didn't want join them in this unfashionable London district and so eventually found somewhere to rent closer to the Sinclair home.

The move coincided with the end of his first year at Guildford. He was due to stay on for another year to complete his course but instead dropped out and spent the summer in France, Belgium and Holland, his first experience of travel outside of Britain. "He obviously had ambitions, but he wasn't sure where they were leading," says Iain. "He was vaguely keen on advertising."

He found work as a messenger boy with Grant Advertising Ltd. in Grosvenor Street in London's West End, probably in the summer of 1960. Grant Advertising Inc. had started in Chicago in 1935 and by 1959 had 42 offices worldwide, the largest network of wholly owned advertising agency offices. Among its major US clients were Mars, Bendix Aviation, Dr. Pepper and Chrysler.

Opposite: Stanley and Rosina Meaden. It wasn't until late in his life that Peter was told that Stanley was not his biological father. The effect was devastating

He began to socialise with young advertising executives in pubs like the Bunch of Grapes in Knightsbridge. "At the same time we were hanging around in Hampstead," says Iain. "We spent 90 percent of our time chasing women around."

He was also enchanted with the new trends in men's clothing. "He knew all about fashion. You couldn't get much good clothing off the shelf. We used to get our suits made at Burton's and Peter knew what to ask for. God knows where he learned it all! He would know there was a thing called flair line with waisted suits and later on we'd get hipster trousers. John Michael opened a boutique on King's Road that was the start of the ready-to-wear fashion revolution."

It was between Peter's arrival in Hampstead in 1960 and the opening of The Scene club in Ham Yard in 1963 that the elements of the mod image, lifestyle and outlook on life began to coalesce. He was already dressing sharply but his hair was still combed back off his forehead and his shirts were colourfully American. He'd yet to be affected by the more sophisticated and understated elements of French and Italian style.

The Guardian reported on the emergence of 'modernists' in a 1960 story on music sessions taking place each lunchtime at the Lyceum Ballroom in Covent Garden. Every day an average of 850 young people were dancing to records and showing off their latest clothes, much of which was made by tailors, mothers, and custom shoemakers. Gentlemen entering the Lyceum were instructed to wear ties and jackets. Jeans and leather jackets were banned. Maybe this rule influenced the smart mod styles. "What is modernist?" the writer asked. "It means you wear an Italian suit with narrow trousers, pointed shoes, and have a flat haircut." [1]

Sometime in 1961 he met Gina Strauss an elfin-like 15-year old South African with paternal Hungarian origins who had arrived in England in 1951 with her mother, brother and sister and was

Opposite: Gina Strauss was the wayward teenage daughter of a wealthy Hampstead family. Peter met her in 1961

1 Wall, Michael, Lunchtime at the Lyceum, The Guardian, February 24 1960

This page and opposite: Peter in the garden of the Meaden family home in Cuthbert Road, Edmonton, 1960

living in a large house on Langland Gardens in Hampsead. Her father, who had recently deserted the family, was a wealthy Cape Town hotelier. She was well spoken, had been educated at The King Alfred School in Golders Green (an independent day school) and was interested in music and film. To onlookers she epitomised the young upper-class beatnik with her black hair, white lipstick and dark eye shadow. Slim, mysterious, and bewitching, she offered the promise of entrance to a world far more exotic than anything he'd known in Farnham. Susie Orbach remembers her as "lovely and enthusiastic."

"There were two girls that we picked up one night in Hampstead," recalls Iain. "I don't remember the name of mine, but Peter's was Gina and she was a lovely girl. They were close for a long time. I think she introduced him to a good crowd because she lived in a good area. That was important in enabling him to get to know new people. She didn't have a father around, just her mum, and they were a bit alternative in the way they lived."

Peter had by now left his job as a messenger and was working as an assistant in the four-man marketing department of Armstrong Warden, an advertising agency and media consultancy at 69 New Oxford Street, close to Tottenham Court Road. A slightly older colleague, Ian Maitland, remembers that their salaries were around £12 a week. "But on that I could buy suits from good tailors, eat out regularly in Soho restaurants and run an old bread van."

Here Peter got hands-on knowledge of everything from page layouts to market research and he was excited to be working in such a creative atmosphere although not so excited by the actual accounts that ranged from soap powder packaging and Schick Razors to advising The Ministry of Health on the effectiveness of anti-smoking campaigns. He was introduced to AC Nielsen's analysis of consumer market shares and took part in runs to Brighton where they would stop at every chemist's shop to see how much of client Richard Hudnut's shampoo was being stocked. This method of research would stand him in good stead in the record industry.

Being close to London's West End meant that he was better able to frequent the clubs of Soho and inspect all the latest American and Continental style clothes appearing in shops like Cecil Gee and Austin's on Shaftesbury Avenue, Vince Man's Shop in Great Newburgh Street, and Sportique on Old Compton Street. He graduated from cider to beer. For a short while he rented a rundown flat on the top floor of a building in Frith Street that only had a basin on the landing to wash in.

During September and October 1961 he and Gina visited the Everyman frequently for its season of Nouvelle Vague films that included *Les Cousins* by Chabrol, *La Quatre Cents Coups* by Truffaut and *Hiroshima Mon Amour* by Renais. He loved the cool nonchalance of the French actors who wore well-cut suits and smart shirts and smoked with aplomb. It was during one of these screenings that Peter met someone who would change the direction of his life.

Andrew Loog Oldham, a shade over two years his junior, was the product of a dalliance between a single English girl and an American serviceman. Unlike Peter's biological father, the airman known as Andrew Loog had not survived the war. He had been shot down over the English Channel six months before his son's birth. Less introverted than Peter, Oldham had a similar resistance to formal education and a fascination with American pop culture. He was also an effective hustler who thrived on spotting new trends and figuring out ways to market them. He had already worked in a men's clothing store, window dressed for fashion designer Mary Quant, sold imported pop singles and been featured in the *Evening Standard's* Mainly for Men column (September 25 1962) in a story about the demise of the striped shirt. McGill described him simply as "a very sharp dresser" and Oldham spoke about repurposing his old school shirts. "They are thick grey cotton. I hated them at school but almost overnight they are marvellous. Whoever would have thought it!"[2]

Mainly for Men was written by a 34-year old gay journalist, Angus McGill, who'd been hired by the Standard editor Charles Wintour to keep his finger on the pulse of young London. Wintour's daughter Anna, later to become the legendary editor of the US edition of *Vogue*, was about to enter her teens and Charles was aware that great changes were afoot. Even though McGill was old in terms of the generation he had been entrusted with covering, he had a good eye, an attentive ear and impeccable taste.

In April 1962 McGill had written one of the most detailed pieces so far about the style of modernists in which he started by saying that "Whether you liked [the Teddy Boy] or not, he's gone now. He's not been killed off by outraged society. He's just been overtaken by changing fashions. So what have we in his place? We have the modernist, that's what we have. And we might as well get used to him. He's likely to be around for a while."

The height of male modernist fashion in 1962, according to McGill, was "a suit called the Sackville" devised by two tailors in Clapham Junction named Brian and Richard. The Sackville had a shortish waisted jacket with sloping shoulders, thin lapels, narrow pocket flaps, deep vents and trousers with 17-inch bottoms, no turn-ups and no raised seams. Shirts had "high Sinatra collars" with long three-inch points. Jackets were often cut low at the neck to better show off the shirt collar. Winkle pickers were by now "rarely seen". Carnaby Street was mentioned. Interestingly, none of the stories about modernists so far defined them by their musical tastes, or drug habits. It was all about clothes.

Although both Peter and Oldham were interested in music

Opposite: Angus McGill kept his finger on the pulse of young London writing the Mainly for Men column in the Evening Standard

2 McGill, Angus, Sorry Chaps - Stripes Are on the Way Out, London, *Evening Standard*, September 25, 1962

their choices were not noticeably daring or niche for the era. Peter liked Ricky Nelson and Dion. Oldham liked Elvis and the Everly Brothers. The greater bond was one of style, image and a fascination with hipster culture. Just as Peter ploughed through William Shirer's *The Rise and Fall of Third Reich* not out of any serious interest in Nazism but because he thought Hitler knew a thing a two about mass media, so Andrew collected jazz records not because he loved jazz but because he admired the artwork on the LP covers being produced by companies such as Blue Note, Columbia, RCA Victor, Verve, Prestige and Dial. "We honed each other's humour, band-aided each other's social sores and fronted the lot with the totality of that," Oldham wrote in his book *Stoned*. "Peter had been out and about longer than I, so I happily fed off his learning."

In June 1962 Peter travelled to the Cote d'Azur to link up with Oldham who'd decided to take an extended break from England and shuttle between St Tropez, Cannes, Antibes, Nice and Monte Carlo, living largely by his wits. When they reunited Oldham was involved in a scam with *Daily Express* stringer Peter Kinsley and society photographer Philip Townsend. They invented the story that Caroline Ford, a socialite on holiday in Monte Carlo, had eloped with Oldham. Townsend got the first pictures of the scandalous couple, of course, and Kinsley got the story. They earned £300 from feeding titbits to gossip columnists back in the UK.

This was one of the first examples of Oldham's talent to mess with the press and to play with the British penchant for loving to hate misbehaviour. Peter wrote a postcard to his parents and brother Gerald: "Sorry I have not written before, but my photographer mate and I have been working on a newspaper story which turned out to be a big thing. Terrifically exciting. Have been to villas for photo sessions of Somerset Maugham (and) Marc Chagall the painter. Going to dinner on a yacht at Monte Carlo tonight. Be home shortly – about a week."

Peter and Oldham decided to pool their talents to produce brochures for companies and PR for individuals although, curiously, Oldham appears to have simultaneously maintained his own portfolio, doing publicity for Decca artists such as Jess Conrad on his single 'Pretty Jenny', dancer Peppi (Borza) on 'Stories' (produced by Shadows' drummer Tony Meehan) and Kenny Hollywood on 'Magic Star' (produced by Joe Meek). He also worked on records by Bryan Hyland, Mark Wynter and Chris Montez and a UK tour starring Sam Cooke and Little Richard. He was brash, inventive and opportunistic, mingling easily with both stars and journalists. He thought nothing of inveigling his way into the presence of stars like Shirley Bassey by tracking down their home addresses and turning up on their doorsteps to offer his services.

It's difficult to imagine what he thought Peter could add to this already successful process and to work out how he segregated the Andrew Loog Oldham projects from the Image projects. They used the printing facilities of Armstrong Warden to create fliers that were then sent out to clothing manufacturers and stores in the hopes of picking up work. In August 1962 their local paper, *The Hampstead and Highgate Express*, reported on their progress in a short diary note that already bears the hallmarks of the boys' aptitude for spin.

"The hazards of the advertising world, which have led to New York's Madison Avenue being nicknamed Ulcer Gulch, appear to have few terrors for 19-year old Andrew Loog Oldham and Peter Meaden.

"A year ago these two former public schoolboys (sic) founded their own advertising and public relations firm, The Image Design Unit.

"And already they handle advertising for an American manufacturing company, dress shops and an office machinery firm, and look after publicity for a group of actors, singers and photographers.

"They share a flat and office in Netherhall Gardens, Hampstead, and, according to Mr. Oldham, have some other ventures in mind.

"'Things are going pretty well, and we're reasonably satisfied,' he said.

"Having made such progress so quickly, they deserve to be."

They were both becoming such masters of the art of hype that it's difficult to sift the facts from the froth. What was the 'American manufacturing company' and why would it employ two lads working out of a North London flat to 'handle' its advertising? Perhaps this was a reference to someone that Peter was already dealing with at Armstrong Warden. There's a possibility that the 'dress shops' were those owned by the designer, Mary Quant, inventor of the mini-skirt.

The piece roughly coincided with Peter's departure from Armstrong Warden by which time Image had its own headed notepaper proclaiming that it dealt in 'Advertising. Design. Public Relations.' On September 8, 1962, Peter wrote to Iain Sinclair outlining the recent changes in his life;

"Dear Iain,

"How are you buddy boy? A lot has happened since I last heard from you. I left my job at Armstrong-Warden's 3 weeks ago to start up full time the advertising agency – see clipping from the Ham and High Express. Things are going fantastically. Making pots of money. Had a super holiday in the South of France and came back all bronzed à la Steve Reeves[1]. I met this Canadian chap, Claude, who has been bumming round Europe and S of F for last 7 months and he came back to London with me. We've got ourselves a terrific studio/penthouse flat in Hampstead and things are going so fine it's just not true. Anyway, we are holding a really wild party on Saturday 16th Sept - Saturday after next, AND YOU'VE GOT TO COME – definitely. I've got so much to let you in on etc. etc. OUR ADDRESS: TOP FLAT 16, ELLERDALE ROAD,

Opposite: Letter from Peter to Iain Sinclair on Image headed paper. The Netherhall gardens address was Andrew Oldham's London home

3 Steve Reeves (1926-2000), American bodybuilder and actor.

IMAGE

IMAGE DESIGN UNIT

19, Netherhall Gardens
Hampstead
London · N·W·3

Telephone SWiss Cottage 2017

ADVERTISING · DESIGN · PUBLIC RELATIONS

8th September 1962.

Dear Iain,

How are you, buddy boy? A lot has happened since I last heard from you. I left my job at Armstrong – Jardens 3 weeks ago to start up full time the advertising agency — see clipping from the Ham & High Express — Things are going fantastically — making pots of money! Had a super holiday in the South of France & came back all bronzed, à la Steve Reeves. I met this Canadian chap, Claude, who has been bumming round Europe & S. of F. for past 7 months & he came back to London with me. We've got ourselves a terrific studio/penthouse flat in Hampstead and things are going so fine its just not true. Anyway we are holding a really wild party on Saturday 16th Sept — Saturday after next, AND YOU'VE GOT TO COME – definitely. I've got so much to let you in on etc etc

OUR ADDRESS: TOP FLAT 16, ELLERDALE ROAD, HAMPSTEAD, N.W.3

Make sure you come — O.K. — & bring a bottle of wine — if you feel like coming up best earlier — come on — we'll put you up — but not this week-end tho' — I'll be away until Sunday remember — I don't work now — so anytime of day or night Yours Pete.

Peter Meaden · Andrew Loog Oldham

HAMPSTEAD N. W. 3. Make sure you come – O. K. – and bring a bottle of wine – if you feel like coming up here earlier – come on – we'll put you up – but not this weekend though – I'll be away until Sunday and remember – I don't work now – so any time or day or night.

"*Yours, Peter.*"

The same month Marc Bolan – then Mark Feld of Stamford Hill – appeared in the stylish gentleman's magazine *Town* in a feature titled 'The Young Take the Wheel' with the strap line "Young men who live for clothes and pleasure." This story is now generally recognised as the first major media acknowledgement of the mod movement but the text by 'Peter Barnsley' (actually moonlighting *Evening Standard* columnist Angus McGill, who clearly had his ear to the ground) notably didn't use the word mod. It also made no mention of music or drugs. The lads profiled were just sharply dressed young men who obsessed about the way they looked and prided themselves on being two steps ahead of the crowd. Bolan was apparently mortified when the issue finally hit the stands seven months after photographer Donald McCullin had pictured him with his two friends because, true to form, they'd already moved on.

The first job Image took on appears to have been the designing of invitations to the launch of the latest John Michael menswear outlet at 83 New Bond Street. They both admired the original John Michael shop in the King's Road and the smaller outlet Sportique in Old Compton Street, Soho, so Oldham found the home address of owner John Michael Ingram and paid him an unscheduled visit. The commission came as a result. Image was then asked to design the next spring brochure for Sportique and they set about cannibalising fashion spreads from the American magazine *Esquire* and created a storyboard where film director 'Ted Wayne' goes driving on the Riviera and picks up blond hitchhiker 'Lance' who's kitted out in Sportique summer shorts. Ingram rejected the artwork because of its gay

Opposite: Part of Town's *September 1962 spread on nascent London mods (although the word 'mod' wasn't used) featuring Mark Feld (bottom right) who would later become a star with T. Rex as Marc Bolan*

y appear. Perhaps the girls are really quite
... that some square and ordinary young
... exist — a world peopled entirely by faces
... be a nightmare.

... is the most remarkable of the three
... he is five years younger than either of
... other two and appears to have no visible
... of support. His father is a lorry-driver
... his mother works in Berwick Market; she
... joined there by her son on Saturdays when he
... in a full day's work. Otherwise the week
... to bend and stretch to his will, extending
... days into the nights and telescoping the
... Sundays into a brief sleep. In common
... the others his conversation only be-
... animated when asked about his clothes.
... says, 'I've got ten suits, eight sports
... fifteen pairs of slacks, thirty to thirty-
... good shirts, about twenty jumpers, three
... jackets, two suède jackets, five or six
... of shoes and thirty exceptionally good ties.'
... Sugar has a Polish father and a sister
... owns a hairdressing salon in Hornsey,
... he works as her assistant. 'I'm 20 and I
... home about £12 a week. Sometimes a bit
... I give my mum 50s a week and the rest
... Most of it goes on clothes. Clothes and
...

... he and Michael Simmonds, who also
... at hairdressing in the New North Road,
... been cutting each other's hair for years
... joke about their work a good deal. 'I sent
... women out today the same colour as they
... in' (this must be largely the woman's
... if she can't tell the colour of her own
... 'and I've got varicose veins already from
... ing all day long.'

... is definitely the leader of the group. As
... of them has a car it is he who organises
... from acquaintances on their complicated
... London evenings. Once used, the hapless
... of the car will be lucky if he is allowed
... the party or stay with the boys at all;
... simply made into a convenience and then
... ten.

... Simmonds is the quietest and most
... tive and has some regularity in his life:
... Friday night he has supper with his aunt
... sets her hair for her afterwards. He is
... gly influenced by Peter, who likes to be
... spokesman on every possible occasion, but
... prepared to reveal that he, like the others,
... ambitions whatsoever. 'I'd like to travel,
... go to Africa' is all he will say.

... parents seem to be unaffected by their
... control over the children. Perhaps it
... their initial lack of interest that caused
... to be as they are, but the present situa-
... summed up by Mark Feld's mother.
... irons his shirts himself. I can't do them
... well.'

... got to be different from the other kids,'
... Feld. 'I mean you got to be two steps
... The stuff that half the haddocks you
... around are wearing I was wearing years
... kid in my class came up to me in his
... it, an Italian box it was, he says "Just

subtext and Image didn't get paid for its effort.

In December 1962 Bob Dylan visited London for the first time to play a role in a one-off BBC TV drama, *Madhouse on Castle Street*, and to check out the British folk scene at venues like Bunjies off Charing Cross Road and The Troubadour in Earls Court. Oldham came across Dylan's manager Albert Grossman in a West End hotel and the upshot was he was invited to be press agent for a week for a £5 fee. At the time Dylan was a virtual unknown in the UK (he'd only recorded one album) but Oldham managed to get him some coverage. Peter didn't have much to do with this small campaign yet referred to it for the rest of his life.

This was the period during which drugs entered his life. For some reason he couldn't cope with the strain of the Sportique commission and he suffered a minor breakdown. He went to his family doctor, Iris Krass, complaining of anxiety and was prescribed Drinamyl, a drug in tablet form containing both amphetamine and barbiturate manufactured by Smith, Kline & French for the alleviation of anxiety and depression. They were also used to help women lose weight. As soon as he started taking the drug he felt free and believed that it offered him a new lease on life.

These small triangular tablets – known as Purple Hearts or Frenchies to those in the know – were not then part of a lifestyle choice. They were simply an aid to carrying on a normal life. Musicians used them to stay awake when playing late night gigs. Harassed housewives used them to cope with boredom. Harold Macmillan is believed to have taken them during the Suez Crisis. He wasn't joining a youth subculture of pill swallowers.

Opposite: The 1962 drama Madhouse on Castle Street *brought Bob Dylan to London. Andrew Oldham got him his first UK press*

On January 13, 1963, Oldham accompanied Mark Wynter to a recording of the popular TV programme *Thank Your Lucky Stars* at the Alpha Television Studios in Aston, Birmingham. At the bottom of a bill that included Acker Bilk, Petula Clarke and

the Brook Brothers were The Beatles, performing their second single 'Please Please Me'. Andrew got talking to their manager Brian Epstein and before the end of the day had been appointed as The Beatles' press representative in London while the group, Epstein and NEMS Enterprises remained in Liverpool.

Image, the company, was now underperforming and Peter and Oldham were going their own separate ways. Oldham was renting office space in Regent Street from Eric Easton, an old music business hand, and making an impression on everyone with his well-cut suits, dark glasses and fancily cut hair. Peter was finding it hard to keep up with his energetic junior. He shared Oldham's sharp eye and both men had their fingers on the pulse of the times, but Peter had no follow-through. He didn't have the toughness or persistence necessary to survive.

On February 23 1958 the *Daily Mirror* published 'Are You a Trad or a Mod?' by Anne Allen. The 'trads' had beards and jived at The Cy Laurie Jazz Club whereas mods wore neckties and went to The Flamingo. On March 2, 1963 the *Mirror* ran the similarly titled 'Mod or Trad?', written by Shirley Lowe. Mod men, she observed, "used to patronise the Italian style, with short jackets and short hair, but have now gone over to college-boy hairstyles, well-cut mohair suits, and slim knitted ties…"

In February 1964 Mavis Davidson wrote a full-page feature on Carnaby Street for the *Daily Herald* which was headlined 'The Mecca for the Mods' in which she detailed the mod search to be ahead of the times. "In a world so urgent that tomorrow is already out of date, the Mods were, perhaps, inevitable," she said. "For the creed of mod is the creed of the conveyor belt. A perpetual motion in which to stop is to cease. To be a mod yesterday is not to be a Mod. It is a world which does not admit the past tense. And which regards the present with suspicion. It is a world which creates its own trends. A feeling, a mood which recognizes suddenly that something is right, and then, in obedience to itself, as suddenly destroys it."

Opposite: Keith Moon and Pete Townshend dancing at The Scene club, 1964. Peter Meaden is behind Townshend

Three years earlier, in his book *The Big Beat Scene*, the pop music journalist, poet and pundit of teenage taste, Royston Ellis, had spotted what he called "the clean-cut modern manner" being exhibited in Soho coffee bars. He described a typical boy; "His brown hair is short, trimmed crisp and parted college-boy style, growing straight down his neck to his collar...His clothes are typical of the teenage trend. He is well-dressed, smart in a striped jacket...His trousers – a grey kind of check with fifteen-and-a-half inch bottoms – are pressed to a razor edge crease. His shirt is one of those dark green flannel efforts buttoned at the neck. He wears no tie."

On March 9, 1963 Oldham joined The Beatles as they toured Britain on a bill headlined by the hit-makers Tommy Roe ('Sheila') and Chris Montez ('Let's Dance'). The Beatles' progress was so fast that no sooner had the tour begun than they replaced the American stars as the top billing act. The tour finished in Leicester on March 31 by which time Peter had left for Spain intending to travel on to Montreal after a holiday to link up with his Canadian friend Claude. However, the air ticket that Claude sent him proved to be invalid and so he changed his plans and stayed on in Spain.

His infrequent letters back home reveal him to have been adrift, and uncertain of what to do next. He stayed at a cheap pension on Calle de Luna in the Malasana district of Madrid and planned to survive by teaching conversational English to local Spaniards for an hour a day. He appears to have spent most of his time eating, drinking and sunbathing with occasional forays to nightclubs where he listened to flamenco guitarists. In April he went to Seville for Semana Santa, or Holy Week, where he was impressed by the street processions with their huge floats carrying sacred works of art and saw his first bullfight ("It is the most dangerous game in the whole world. I am a convicted fan.") The next month he went to the annual film festival in Cannes. He was naturally drawn to spectacle, imagery and ritual.

Opposite: In his book The Big Beat Scene *Royston Ellis had identified boys showing "the clean cut modern manner" in Soho coffee bars back in 1961*

42

In his early letters he appeared full of confidence, talking about his lack of financial worries and the cheapness of Spanish life. He likened the atmosphere of Madrid to that of interwar Paris when Hemingway, Fitzgerald and company held court in the cafes of St. Germain. His parents though remained worried that their 21-year old son still hadn't knuckled down either to a serious course of study or to a promising career and he ended almost every letter by assuring them that they had no grounds for concern. At one point he sharply reprimanded his mother; "Mum, do stop sending those boring letters about settling down, responsibilities etc. I know exactly what I am doing."

Later a note of desperation began to creep in. "You could send a few quid" (April 29), "Sell the motorbike if you can" (May 17), "I would be much obliged if you could arrange to let me have as much of that £10 you got for the motorbike as soon as you can" (June 18), "I lost all my savings (about £18) on the beach... About £5-£6 would get me out of the position I'm in at present... Sorry to have to ask you but you're the only one I can depend on and I do need it..." (July 10).

Gerald Meaden believes that it was bad debts rather than a lust for travel that caused him to leave England in the first place. "Something went wrong in his partnership with Andrew," he says. "They tried to start a business for free newspapers in the Hampstead area and it got out of hand. They couldn't finance it properly. Andrew disappeared for a while as well."

This is partly borne out by one sharply worded letter in which he castigates his mother for trying to deal with an unpaid bill on his behalf. He didn't want her opening his mail and discovering his financial problems. "Just received letter re. Queensway Press. DON'T, repeat don't, pay it. This matter I will arrange from this end. I don't want you interfering and especially paying out money for things you have no knowledge of. It is nothing to do with you and they cannot do anything to you. So, don't pay anything to anyone who writes to ME. Understand? ... As I am over 21 you cannot be held in any way responsible for matters such as this. I will arrange for the matter to be cleared up. OK?"

He never mentioned PR or advertising in the letters and the only music referred to was what he'd heard played on guitars in the late-night cafes and a song he'd co-written with an American traveller he'd just met. He was continuing to draw and even to paint. He spoke vaguely of going into business with someone planning to run a bar in Majorca, toyed with the idea of driving through Africa in a Land Rover and then told his mother, almost certainly to butter her up, that he was considering returning to art school to complete his diploma and possibly going on to the Royal College of Art (presumably to do a post-graduate course).

When he arrived back at the end of July 1963 London was in full swing. In Peter's absence The Beatles had released their first LP, the London Tourist Board had been established, John Profumo had resigned from the Cabinet over his affair with escort Christine Keeler, *Glamour* magazine had voted Jean Shrimpton Model of the Year, and the old chart dominance by first generation rock 'n' rollers and mainstream pop stars was being effectively challenged by new 'beat' groups from the north of England like Billy J. Kramer and The Dakotas, Gerry and The Pacemakers and The Searchers.

Most galling for Peter was the fact that while he'd been sitting it out in the sunshine Andrew Oldham's career had taken off in an even bigger way. At the end of April, acting on a tip-off from *Record Mirror* journalist Peter Jones, he'd come across The Rolling Stones at the Crawdaddy Club in Richmond, formed a company he named Impact Sound to manage them along with Eric Easton (being under 21 he needed an older associate to sign contracts), secured the Stones a record deal with Decca and had seen their first single ('Come On') recorded. All this had happened over a two-week period. By the time Peter got back to England 'Come On' was in the Top Thirty.

He anticipated that he would be offered work, possibly co-managing the Stones, but due to his unreliability and lack of business skills Oldham couldn't see a natural role for him in the organisation. This was now serious business and Peter was too high a risk. He tried unsuccessfully to wheedle a job out of Brian Epstein but Epstein, even though he was gay, found Peter too flamboyant for his liking.

"They'd had a falling out," says photographer Philip Townsend of the relationship between Peter and Oldham. "I think Peter tried to copy Andrew, but he just couldn't do it. He didn't have the gift. They were very similar in what they wore, but one was a genius and the other wasn't." Peter took his revenge by having 2000 stickers made up offering the sexual services of an experienced madam, with Andrew's business phone as the contact number, and posting them in central London public conveniences. This successfully tied up the office phone for almost three weeks.

Oldham offloaded Peter on to Townsend who had a photographic studio at 51 Brompton Road and was doing a lot of society shoots for *The Tatler*. "Andrew was just a bit fed up with him because he was always moaning and not doing very much so he said to me, 'You can have him.' He didn't really know what he wanted to do so we started Townsend, Meaden & Partners, that was an agency that supplied bands. We offered what we called 'the very best in beat music' for debutante dances."

With Townsend's contacts in the British upper class they were soon spending nights in Park Lane hotels, English country houses and exclusive venues in areas like Chelsea and Hampstead while unknown bands such as The Starliners and Gene Russell and The Renegades entertained the new breed of young aristocrats who favoured the twist and the shimmy over the waltz and the foxtrot.

One of their most popular acts was Peter Asher and Gordon Waller, then billed as Gordon and Peter (later to become

Opposite: Philip Townsend was a society photographer who briefly went into business with Peter offering music acts for debutante balls and country house parties

46

successful EMI recording artists as Peter and Gordon). The two teenage boys had met at the top independent London school, Westminster, and Peter's sister, Jane, was a prominent actress as well as the girlfriend of Paul McCartney. On the launch bill in Chelsea on November 16, 1963 they not only appeared in their own right as a duo but Gordon, in disguise, came on during the first half as 'Aubyn St. Clair' and early during the second as 'Marc Conquest'. Jane Asher was in attendance.

They got some coverage in the *Daily Herald* where youth columnist Henry Fielding mentioned not only 'Aubyn St. Clair' ("intelligent" and "former head boy" of Westminster School) but 'pop poet' Hessian Boots and artist Toni Litri who "refuses to exhibit his works unless there is suitable music at the same time to complete his paintings." He quoted Townsend as saying; "Denmark Street is turning out stereotype singers and groups. Ours are very different."

The two of them also set up a short-lived PR company, Townsend-Meaden PR. They met with designers Cecil and Lee Bender, later to form the successful Kensington boutique Bus Stop, but didn't get the account. "Peter had met them somewhere and they were interested in us doing something for them," says Townsend. "We went to a meeting with them and following that they told us we didn't have enough experience."

Yet despite the setbacks Peter's brief life was about to enter its golden age. He'd got the style and the drugs, now he was to encounter the music, ambience and community that would draw these apparently random elements together. While he was away in Spain a small basement club, The Scene, had started at 41 Great Windmill Street (the entrance was actually in Ham Yard), just a few yards away from Piccadilly Circus. The venue itself was nothing out of the ordinary – it had a long history as a bohemian hangout, most recently had been operating as Cy Laurie's Jazz Club – but the music it played was extraordinary for the era. Within a short time period it would

Opposite: Handbill for a Chelsea event promoted by Peter and Philip Townsend in 1963. Gordon Waller managed to be Aubyn St. Claire, Marc Conquest and half of 'Gordon & Peter' all on the same show

become the most influential music club in Britain, attracting crowds of fashionable, adventurous young people hungry for authenticity and personal liberation.

The Scene was a business venture by South African accountant Lionel Blake, who had spent the past two years managing La Discotheque in Wardour Street (a club owned by Ukrainian born slum landlord Perec 'Peter' Rachman and Lebanese born gangster Raymond Nakachian aka Raymond Nash of the notorious North London 'Nash Gang'), and Irish financial heir Ronan O'Rahilly. Neither of them had intended to build a mod venue. It was just the way that things had come together, and Peter Meaden was to play a vital role in the creation of the attitude and reputation of the club as exclusive, edgy and innovative.

Soho's clubland of the time was a potent mix of entertainment, crime, sleaze, wealth and corruption. Criminally inclined leaseholders used the ambience of clubs to seduce punters into an underground world where they would be enticed to buy the wares of various pimps, prostitutes, and pushers. They would then take a percentage of the profits earned by these merchants.

Opposite: Ronan O'Rahilly, who ran The Scene club, standing (left) on the bow of the Radio Caroline ship shortly before the station launched on Easter Sunday 1964 – the same weekend as the first mods and rockers skirmishes at Clacton

One worker on Rachman's payroll was also Soho's best-known and best-connected amphetamine dealer, known to everyone as Peter the Pill. It was no surprise that clubs controlled by Rachman were also awash with tablets and that corrupt police officers were taking kickbacks for either turning a blind eye to what was going on or giving advance warnings of raids so that club officials were clean when the men in blue arrived.

Blake's personal taste in music was unashamedly old-fashioned – he liked The Inkspots and musical soundtracks – and having grown up on a remote farm in South Africa he'd had no teenage experience of clubs or subcultures. He knew that he needed the input of other more tuned-in people to make the club a success. "I came from the countryside and here I was at the heart of one of the biggest cities of the world. That's why I

enjoyed it. I was an outsider in the centre of things, and I knew I didn't have the ideas. That's why I got a good team around me."

His first hire was a 23-year old girl named Sandra Blackstone. He picked her because of her beauty – she was an attractive dyed blonde who'd previously worked as a hostess in Soho clubs – but he soon discovered that she had an exquisite taste in music that appealed to young club goers. She played records before the bands went on and had her own recorded-music-only nights during the week advertised as 'Off the Record with Sandra'. "It was only after she'd been with us a few months that I realised that she only ever went out with black American GIs and so she got all the latest records from them," says Blake. "She knew exactly what to play and when to play it. Early in the evening she'd play fun things and then later on she'd play the heavy stuff. She had all the special records that no one else in England had copies of."

Sandra was a mysterious yet influential figure. Almost no one knew her surname and even Blake, who did, knew nothing about her background. He didn't know that she was born in Portsmouth as Sandra Lane in 1939 and had come to London and married at the age of 20 to Cyril Blackstone, the brother of the lyricist Don Black who would go on to write the words for such celebrated songs as 'Thunderball', 'Diamonds Are Forever', 'Born Free' and 'Love Changes Everything.'

She'd had a troubled childhood. Her parents went through an acrimonious divorce when she was nine and her mother was awarded custody after the judge determined that too much access to the father could "poison the child's mind." It's likely that she fled to London as a teenager to put the past behind her but after a very short time together, and the birth of a daughter, Karen, she and Cyril split up. Sandra abandoned her baby, went blonde, disappeared from her family's radar and invented a new life that her former husband wouldn't know about until the writing of this book. The last time he saw her was when she

Opposite: Sandra Blackstone (nee Lane) was an influential DJ at The Scene club. Here she is pictured circa 1962 with her daughter Karen

visited his office in the West End accompanied by a West Indian drug dealer and begged for money to help her start a new life in America.

The next member of The Scene club's staff was another DJ, 20-year old Guy Stevens, who was an obsessive collector of American records from small independent labels based in places like Memphis, Tennessee, and Shreveport, Louisiana. He'd been converted to rock 'n' roll after hearing 'Great Balls of Fire' by Jerry Lee Lewis, had run his school's Rock 'n' Roll Appreciation Society and was now living on a diet of mail order singles and LPs from the labels Sue, Chess and Stax. Like Peter, and Andrew Oldham, he'd not fared well at school (he was expelled at 14) but also like them he had a passion for all things American and was tuned into the tastes of the restless young. "Guy just came down and met us," says Blake. "The club had been running with Sandra alone and then we took him on. He was perfect for what we wanted because our only rule was 'No Top Twenty singles.'"

The specific mod focus developed with Peter, who was as significant a contributor to The Scene in Blake's view as the two record spinners. He came via an introduction from Oldham and Blake took an immediate liking to him. "Peter said to me, 'Lionel. I've got a gimmick for The Scene club.' He used the word 'mod'. He started all that. Before this we'd had a lot of older people coming down and it didn't have a strong identity. He knew a lot about the pop scene and the culture. He knew how the young people thought and felt. That's why I let him do what he wanted."

Peter never acted in an official capacity as a PR for The Scene but he became its primary advocate by drawing in the style-conscious elite, young music business movers and shakers, and also turning on musicians he met to what was happening. Blake can recall him bringing people like Bo Diddley and Chuck Berry down to experience the atmosphere and recommending

Opposite:
Sandra
Blackstone had
unique access
to American
R&B singles
brought to
the UK by US
servicemen

55

the Graham Bond Organization and George Fame and The Blue Flames as acts to play there.

The Scene was nothing to look at – a small, dank cellar with a low ceiling, bare alcoves and dark corners – but it enabled a vibrant experience as the powerful sounds bounced off the walls and ceilings. The favoured tracks were black and American from labels such as King, Okeh, Symbol, Gordy, Sue, Stax and Motown – songs like 'Monkeying Around' by William Bell, 'Monkey Time' by Major Lance, 'Mockingbird' by Inez and Charlie Foxx, and 'So Far Away' by Hank Jacobs.

Ronnie Jones, soon to be managed as a singer by Ronan O'Rahilly, was one on the GIs stationed in the UK who frequented The Flamingo in Wardour Street starting in 1962. "Every black soldier used to bring his own music with him," he says. "Apart from your duffle bag you had a record player and inside your hard case you had all your singles. When I went to Korea there was no American music out there and so we played our own records over the Tannoy system for an hour each day. When soldiers left to return home, they'd leave their records behind."

The fact that The Scene ran all-nighters made Drinamyl rather than alcohol the drug of choice. It kept the dancers awake, appeared to release extra reserves of energy and created a feeling of intimacy where the all the cares of the outside world drifted away. It also dampened down sexual excitement, which in turn encouraged group bonding rather than flirtation, conquest and pairing off.

Opposite: Guy Stevens, Scene Club DJ, and a stack of American import records with which he groomed the musical tastes of London mods

For Peter it felt like a homecoming. It was a hermetically sealed world consisting only of people who felt, dressed and thought like him. The Scene became an escape not only from home but also from the adult world of business, family and responsibility. Here was a community dedicated to nothing more than pleasure through music, style and drugs. The fashion choices of individualists from all over London began to influence each other and settle down into a recognisable

style that became known as mod.

The report of a police raid in 1964 provides the perfect snapshot of the club's demographic. At 02:55 on December 6, 374 teenagers were on the premises. There were two boys for every girl. Most of the boys were aged between 17-18. The girls were mostly 15-18. When the floor was cleared the police found two flick knives, some 'herbal mixture' and ten packets of pills. Seventy-eight teenagers were taken to West End Central Police station for questioning and eventually five of them were charged with possession of illegal drugs. Peter was at least five years older than the average clubber, a fact that may explain why he became so prominent and influential. He was one of the few adults in this predominantly teenage world.

Michael 'Mickey' Tenner was a 16-year old from Stepney, East London, who discovered The Scene at around the same time. He'd left school at 14 to work at the Mayfair Hotel in Stratton Street, not far from the Ritz on Piccadilly. When his shift ended he would wander into Soho and as he mooched around he encountered music at The Flamingo, La Discotheque and Ronnie Scott's Jazz Club. "Then The Scene club happened, and I met Peter and things started to change in my life," he says. "He was one of the first people I could talk to about fashion and music. In my mind the whole mod thing happened at The Scene club with a little bit of what the GIs were doing at The Flamingo with their Ivy League suits and bluebeat hats."

Opposite: Mickey Tenner outside The Scene club which he discovered in 1963 while working at the Mayfair Hotel. "The photo was all staged," says Tenner. "I didn't own a scooter. I drove a Mini"

Peter still drifted back into Andrew Oldham's sphere although he was no longer working with or for him. He befriended the Stones and was present at Decca Studios when they recorded the Berry Gordy song 'Money' for their first EP. He got on particularly well with Brian Jones and took him down to The Scene. Andrew now had offices at Maddox Street, off Regent Street, which he'd moved to from Poland Street despite it offering less space because he thought the word 'Maddox' sounded classier than 'Poland' when it came to headed

notepaper and business cards.

Oldham publicised other acts such as The Crystals and Gene Pitney and without having an official title Peter helped him out. Oldham was building a reputation not only for being hip in dress and speech but also for being a shrewd dealmaker. Peter, on the other hand, was known for being extremely cool and passionate but also a bit of a liability because of his increasing dependence on Drinamyl. He was either very up – talking at a rapid rate – or he was nowhere to be seen. "By the time I had my office in Maddox Street Peter was useless during the day," admits Oldham.

In his biography *Shake It Up Baby!* former *Record Mirror* journalist Norman Jopling recalled; "Andrew was cool, sharp, very bright, very aware; Meaden, two years older, was more artistic, a bit mad, a bit brilliant, always flailing around. But when Meaden was 'on', no-one could touch him. He generated excitement. Fuelled by pills and whiskey, on a roll about his latest scheme, his latest discovery, his latest project, and you'd stand there listening to him with your jaw dropping at the awesome, crazy connections he'd be making. And believe him, too."

Sandy Roberton, who also had an office in Maddox Street where he managed the UK publishing for Chicago's Chess Records, remembers Peter as the archetypal hustler, frantically dashing around and always talking out of the side of his mouth. "He was like Sidney Falco as played by Tony Curtis in the 1957 film *Sweet Smell of Success*. Burt Lancaster plays this major TV guy and Falso was a New York publicist out and about hustling. That was Peter Meaden."

"Peter was always very pleasant but almost permanently on speed," remembers Tony Calder, who worked with Oldham at the time. "He always had this perspiration on his forehead and on his upper lip. He was mentally involved with the company but hardly ever there. You'd ask him to do something and he

Opposite: Music publisher Sandy Roberton, who was later administered his first LSD trip by Peter

would promise to do it saying 'I'm just going out for coffee. I'll be back in five minutes' and you wouldn't see him for another two days.

"It was like a fashion competition between Peter and Andrew. Andrew would always be sharply dressed just in case Peter came in. When he did come in it would be obvious that he'd been up all night and then he'd disappear for ten minutes and come back with a new shirt. They both knew how to buy the best-looking clothes for the least amount of money. That was their game. They were always trying to outsmart each other.

"Because Peter was a red-skinned, red-haired type of guy he had a totally different look to Andrew who had as dark to slightly fair look. They dressed sharply but they dressed differently because of their skin tones and hair colouring. I was sitting there like a country hick thinking 'What's all the fuss about clothes?' I had a pair of trousers and a jacket and didn't care but they took it very seriously."

Oldham wanted the Stones marketed as being the antithesis of John, Paul, George and Ringo. Where The Beatles were amusing and engaging, the Stones would be curt and surly. Where The Beatles were besuited and smart, the Stones would be casual and dishevelled. He wasted no opportunity to float rumours of their taste for spirits, their unsuitability as prospective marriage partners, and their refusal to obey orders. He knew exactly how to drip feed the media's insatiable appetite for scandal. In an age when it was rare to be able to get front-page newspaper coverage on a pop act he got it when the Stones were accused of urinating on a garage forecourt.

Opposite: Tony Calder (right), business partner of Andrew Oldham (left), saw the relationship between Peter and Oldham at close quarters

Peter had a front row seat as Oldham manipulated the papers and turned outrage into free advertising. He also saw how it was possible to promote a group not just as a collection of music makers but also as a lifestyle statement. The Stones, unlike Mark Wynter, Marty Wilde, Tommy Steele and other acts he'd been involved with, were as much about a new way of

behaving and viewing the world as they were about a new style of music. As Oldham would write in the sleeve notes of their debut album; "The Rolling Stones are more than just a group – they are a way of life."

"Andrew took the image of The Beatles and roughed it up a bit for the Stones," explains Calder. "He started this pop icon marketing and planning – the build-up before the release, the pull back and unavailability the moment the record goes in at number one, the new picture with every release, the 16 mm films. Peter was more into design and the look whereas Andrew was the inspiration. He would say something, and I'd put it into effect. There were no marketing teams or focus groups. No bollocks. There was no one telling us we couldn't do it. If we wanted to do it, we did it. Everything was instant."

Ready Steady Go! was the hot new TV show, broadcast live every Friday night from a studio in Holborn. It had started off tentatively – the first show featured Pat Boone introducing a clip from his latest movie and Burl Ives singing 'The Ugly Bug Ball' – but soon picked up on the new R&B influenced groups like the Stones, The Animals, Manfred Mann and Them. The producers scoured clubs all over London to hand out tickets to the coolest looking teenagers and the best dancers. In this way the show broadcast the latest looks and moves to the whole of Britain.

Going to the filming of *Ready Steady Go!* was to become an essential part of Peter's non-stop weekend. As someone working in the music business he was able to get easy access to the green room where artists, journalists, agents, publicists and managers mingled over drinks. Not surprisingly The Scene club became a vital resource for coolly attired participants and some of the show's dance routines with its official dancers would be worked out there with RSG choreographer Patrick Kerr.

The relationship between The Scene club and RSG was reciprocal. Just as the mods were given access to the TV studios

Opposite: Ronnie Jones was an American GI stationed outside London who discovered The Flamingo Club in 1962 and later performed at The Scene when he was managed by Ronan O'Rahilly

so the RSG performers were taken down to The Scene once the shooting was over. "Vicki Wickham (the show's producer) used to bring a lot of the big names on the show down just to listen to the music," remembers Lionel Blake. "She brought people like Ike and Tina Turner, Dusty Springfield and Dionne Warwick down."

One of the most popular featured dancers was 17-year old Sandy Sarjeant from Kensal Green. "Because I was a regular the people running The Scene club let me know that the *Ready Steady Go!* team was coming down to choose people for an audition," she says. "When I got down there it was packed solid. I'd never seen anything like it. It was almost impossible to dance. I didn't see how anything could happen, so I just spent the night dancing as normal but then I got a tap on the shoulder and someone said; 'We'd like to partner you.'

"I was dancing with anyone who was available, but they wanted to partner me with someone they'd noticed in another part of the club. I didn't know him. We danced together and they said, 'Right. We are at the studios in Holborn on such-and-such a date.' There were three couples selected from The Scene club and I went along with this guy Michael and we were the couple that passed the audition."

No doubt inspired by Oldham's success with the Stones Peter envisaged a group that could both reflect the mod style, embody mod aspirations and play music loved by mods. Groups were playing at The Scene club during the week but none of them looked, thought or wrote like mods. Groups like The Animals might have bought some clothes from Carnaby Street, but they were not the sort of people that mods aspired to look like and nor did their songs articulate their outlook on life.

Tony Calder had started out as a DJ at the Ilford Palais and while there he spotted a group from East Ham called the Moments fronted by an amazingly soulful young singer called Steve Marriott. Once the group was ensconced with Oldham

Opposite: The Scene in Ham Yard, Soho, became the heartbeat of mod. It exerted a nationwide influence on dress, dance and musical tastes

Calder took on their management and handed their PR to Peter who began by ensuring that they all dressed in the latest mod clothes.

"Peter had quite a bit of influence on us in that area," says Moments' keyboard layer Allen Ellett. "We used to go to Anello and Davide to get our boots made and our shirts were made at John Stephen's. We'd all have the same style but perhaps in different colours. I think we were a bit out in front at the time. I don't remember any other band dressing like mods.

"Peter was always full of ideas. In fact, he'd get an idea in his mind and he'd then remind you of it every time you saw him. Mentally he was quite slick, but he let himself down with whatever he was taking. On a good day he could be very quick witted but on a bad day he'd be slurring. On those days we didn't know where we stood with him."

It was in March 1964 – specifically on the Easter weekend of March 27-30 – that mods became headline news in Britain. Hosts of them descended on the coastal resort of Clacton to take part in prearranged skirmishes with their subcultural enemies the rockers. Hundreds came on scooters wearing parkas and even more came down from London by train dressed in suits, Fred Perry shirts, striped madras jackets, leather coats, blue beat hats and shades. The coastal town with its promenade, beaches and pier became a stage where both mods and rockers could strut and pose lapping up the scornful stares of middle-aged holidaymakers, straights and police constables. For the first time they could display their power in public and the enormity of these teenage movements and the vast gap between their way of seeing the world and the views of those they regarded as outdated conformists became obvious.

Opposite: Easter Sunday 1964 saw the first seaside disturbances but it wasn't until the next event – six weeks later – that it was described as Mods vs Rockers

Sandy Sarjeant can recall the invasions being casually organised. "You'd be with some people and they'd say that this Bank Holiday it was Brighton or Margate. Then you'd go around the corner and someone else would say it's going to be Clacton

514

Daily Mirror

3d. Monday, March 30, 1964   No. 18,746

'WILD ONES' INVADE SEASIDE—97 ARRESTS

By PAUL HUGHES

THE Wild Ones invaded a seaside town yesterday—1,000 fighting, drinking, roaring, rampaging teenagers on scooters and motor-cycles. By last night, after a day of riots and battles with police, ninety-seven of them had been arrested.

A desperate S O S went out from police at Clacton, Essex, as leather-jacketed youths and girls attacked people in the streets, turned over parked cars, broke into beach huts, smashed windows, and fought with rival gangs.

Police reinforcements from other Essex towns raced to the shattered resort, where fearful residents had locked themselves indoors.

By this time the centre of Clacton was jammed with onrushing teenagers. Traffic was at a standstill.

Fought

The crowd was broken up by police using dogs. Stones, exploded into a fury as the teenagers fought them.

A number of arrests had already been made ... and then the wails and messages sent to parents.

And worried mothers and fathers were beginning to arrive from the London area to try and take their sons and daughters home.

The hard-pressed police were glad to see them go. But last night as things calmed down tempers were explosed with complaints and comments.

By last night the store of strong and changed and conveyence continued.

Thirty-five arrests on police and riots with charges for rowdyism, obstruction and assault are also due. Many used in a face up and disorderly, machines formed and many others in hospital.

Rough

Police said the court hearings would most likely begin today.

The Wild Ones was the title of a Marlon Brando film in which leather-jacketed youths on motor-cycles created havoc in an American town. The film was banned in this country.

They began arriving on Friday and mostly slept rough under the stars. Their leather jackets and tight jeans soon said to mark them out from the rest.

Others used the wide motorway round the town and their fast vehicles and scooters.

Continued on Back Page

Youths in leather jackets help a police officer making inquiries last night into the rampage by gangs of teenagers at the seaside resort of Clacton. A police dog stands by

SUNDAY JOINT SAVED BY WIVES

THERE were no power cuts during the peak "Sunday lunch" period yesterday.

Yet a United Electricity Board spokesman told reporter that out swank of the country were almost unrelieved by the power cuts.

The reason the cut could be avoided, the spokesman said, was because the Board has managed to build up reserves of electricity.

"The full and rhythmical consumption made it possible to meet the demand when every one was cooking Sunday lunch," he said.

The Easter miracle of Alaska

'FEWER THAN 100' DIE

From ALFRED HARDING, New York, Sunday

THE earthquake which savaged Alaska is being described tonight as "The Easter Miracle."

For although the city of Anchorage and other towns on the south coast of Alaska were battered to pieces in seconds, the number of dead is surprisingly low.

Rescuers expect to find many of the victims buried in rubble of wrecked buildings.

But they estimate that the total will not be lower than 100.

Waves

Earlier reports put the death toll at several hundred, but the hundreds are now missing.

Today Hugh Wade, Alaska's acting Governor, said that fewer than 100 were believed to have died.

When the earthquake struck huge tidal waves swept over small fishing villages, engulfing them.

Damage

Most of the earthquake victims died in these places.

From the stricken Alaskan city of Anchorage a Mirror Corres-

PICTURES—PAGES FOUR AND FIVE

or Hastings. So, you just took your pick. I hated the fighting though. It frightened me. I walked away from it."

The Easter fights at Clacton made the newspaper front pages although the initial reports referred to 'scooter gangs' and 'rampaging teenagers on motorcycles' rather than mods and rockers. Comparisons were made with the 1953 film *The Wild Ones* (starring Marlon Brando) in which a motorcycle gang terrifies residents of the small Californian town. It was in later analysis that journalists attached names to the rival groups. The *Daily Mirror's* lead story 'Wild Ones Invade Seaside – 97 Arrests' on March 30, made no mention of mods or rockers but six weeks later when riots took place on the Whitsun weekend its similar front-page coverage 'Wild Ones Beat Up Margate' called the factions 'self-styled Mods and Rockers'.

The fighting, and the press attention, excited Peter. It meant that the subterranean, after-hours cult in which he believed so passionately was at last being noticed and mods were offending the very people he thought deserved to be offended – magistrates, policemen, vicars, bishops, politicians and ordinary lower middle-class people like his parents who lived what he thought were lives of dull mediocrity. He saw them as an invading army.

One of the Margate mods spoke to the authors of the ground-breaking book of interviews with contemporary teenagers, Generation X, which was published in 1964. He was an 18-year old mechanic named John Braden. "Yes, I am a mod and I was at Margate," he said. "I'm not ashamed of it. I wasn't the only one. I joined in a few of the fights. It was a laugh. I haven't enjoyed myself so much in a long time. It was great – the beach was like a battlefield. It was like we were taking over the country.

"You want to hit back at all the old geezers who try to tell us what to do. We just want to show them we're not going to take it. It was like a battlefield. I felt great, part of something important instead of just being something they look down on because you haven't passed GCE."

It was attitudes like this that Peter wanted to see given expression in contemporary music. He was getting his hair cut by a barber called Lionel 'Jack' Marks in the Edgware Road who knew of his music business connections. One day in April 1964 Jack casually mentioned that another of his clients, Helmut Gorden, had a business interest in a West London pop group called The Detours and wondered whether Peter, with his knowledge of record companies, managers, producers and publicists, could check them out. Peter agreed to see them play.

They met at a rehearsal room in Shepherd's Bush (presumably The Goldhawk Social Club in Goldhawk Road) and even though the group wasn't even playing any self-written songs at the time Peter could see the potential in turning them into the focus of the mod movement. They were unformed enough musically to respond to a crash course in R&B and devoid enough of a strong image to respond to a branding exercise. They seemed malleable.

None of them were mods at this point. Keith Moon was a pranksterish fan of The Beach Boys and favoured outrageous clothes. Roger Daltrey, who had founded the group, was a straightforward rocker and a tough guy. John Entwistle was a serious musical student with a daytime job in a tax office and had little interest in fashion. Pete Townshend, an art student in Ealing, was the most style-conscious of the four and knew enough about bohemian forms of dress, art movements, American folk and blues, and urban street gangs to be particularly interested in the plan to connect with mods.

With a budget of £50 Peter set about kitting them out in some current mod styles as he had done with the Moments. "I rebelled against being made to dress like mods," John Entwistle told me in 1975. "I felt we should have dictated fashion. He took us around these shops and had us dressed in skating jackets, t-shirts, jeans with one -inch turn-ups and boxing boots. Roger was given an Ivy League seersucker suit I walked through a puddle in my boxing boots and the soles fell off."

They were taken to Jack the barber who brought in Philip Andronicos (later dubbed Phil The Greek), a stylish 19-year old hairdresser working in a nearby salon, to give them shorter mod haircuts. "Jack was just an old-fashioned barber," explains Philip. "He had no idea what mods or rockers wanted. He couldn't look at someone and tell what haircut would be best for them. They were happy with what I gave them. It was a modish look but don't ask me what the style was!"

Then Peter took them to meet Guy Stevens in his one room apartment in Leicester Square. Guy had one of the most revered collections of R&B records in London and it became his duty – for £5 – to bring the group up to speed with the latest sounds thrilling the mods at The Scene club. He'd already made up tapes of goodies for the Stones and The Animals and would do so for the Spencer Davis Group. He was the connoisseur of cool. Guy played them Link Wray's 'Rumble', James Brown's 'Please, Please, Please' and a collection of singles from the Motown, Stax and Sue labels. He made a two-and-a-half-hour compilation tape for them. Years later he told Charles Shaar Murray of *NME*: "They were really weird. They just stood there. My wife made a cup of tea for each one of them and they still stood still... I'm playing the records going, 'Jesus Christ! WAKE UP.'"

Peter decided to write both sides of their first single because he wanted the songs to articulate the feelings of a typical Scene Club player and to be an intrinsic part of the mod packaging. As he wasn't a musician he took the basic music structures of two singles from Guy Stevens' collection and penned his own words. The A Side, based on Slim Harpo's 'I Got Love If You Want It' was 'I'm The Face', a song of male mod braggadocio that referenced The Scene, white buckskin shoes and Ivy League jackets. A face was a mod with magnetism and instant recognition who could command a room through style. A face walked the right way,

Opposite: James Brown's 'Please,Please, Please' was played to The Who by Guy Stevens. They would record a version of it for their debut album My Generation

dressed the right way and was always one step ahead of the game. "We said we weren't going to be 'mods'," remembers Mickey Tenner. "We were going to be 'faces'. It was an extension of the mod thing. He wrote the song and I sang backing vocals!"

The B-side, based on 'Misery' by The Dynamics, was 'Zoot Suit', another song about fashion that expands on the role of the face as style leader. He's the 'hippest number' and the 'snappiest dresser' and his message is 'you gotta be cool'. There are intimations of a three-tier hierarchy in the mod kingdom with the majority being mere 'tickets', an inner circle being 'numbers' and the rulers being 'faces'. He even came up with a name for the group that had recently switched from being The Detours to The Who. He wanted them to be known as The High Numbers. For the teenage magazines this would suggest chart aspirations but for the mod elite it would indicate that they were numbers who liked to be high. It was a smuggled drug reference.

Allen Ellett recalls that the group rehearsed the two songs at the Wigmore Hall in Wigmore Street before recording them at Fontana's studio in Stanhope Place near Marble Arch, close to Jack's barber shop. "Peter was trying to get ideas over to them. He would suggest lines that he wanted changing. To be honest they were a bit unruly and had strong ideas of their own but they could see he was doing it with their best interests in mind.

Opposite: The Dynamics, whose B-side 'Misery' provided the template for The High Numbers' 'Zoot Suit' written by Peter Meaden with mods in mind

"I was there at the recording as well. I played a little upright piano. It was a pretty lively scene in the studio with different people coming and going. For one of the tracks Peter took his leather belt off, folded it in two and asked me to crack it like a whip every time the beat came in."

Despite all these well worked out plans, the resource of Guy Stevens' record collection and Peter's familiarity with marketing and image, the two songs didn't bottle the dynamism of their subject matter. Mods were forward-looking, but these tracks sounded like something that a mediocre Merseybeat band

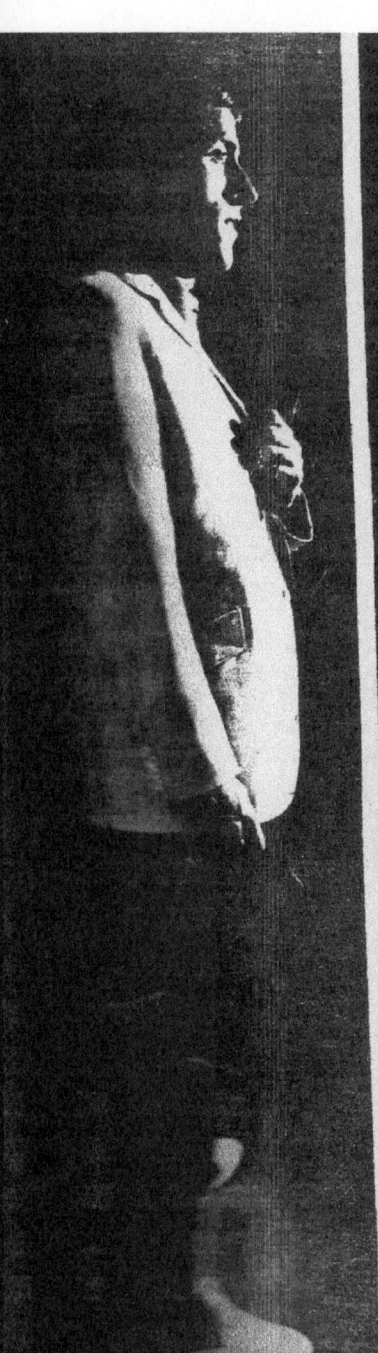

on their first disc outing,

four hip young men

from london say:

i'm the face

and wear:

zoot suit

(the first <u>authentic</u> mod record)

the four hip young men?

the high numbers

fontana tf 480
release date july 3rd 1964

could have come up with. However, faulty as they were, they contained the seeds of everything that would one day make The Who great. Pete Townshend's best material, from 'I Can't Explain' and 'My Generation' to *Tommy* and *Quadrophenia*, came from getting into the mindset of disgruntled, disenfranchised, spiritually confused young people and putting their hopes and frustrations into sounds and words.

Peter Meaden's genius was in paying attention to every aspect of a band from their shoes and haircuts to their lyrics and music in order to ensure a interlocking whole. He also saw the value in having a band spearhead a subcultural revolution in the way that Malcolm McLaren would do a decade later with punk and the Sex Pistols.

"I really related quite strongly to the thematic image building that was going on," admits Pete Townshend. "I'd seen it from the outside with the Stones' kind of raunchy non-image and The Beatles' clean-cut image. Having a defined image, some kind of look, was something that fitted in with my art school thinking.

"When Peter came along with this mod idea I liked it because it had to do with the street and the kids I'd been brought up with and went to school with. I could relate to it. It felt natural. I'd always thought of rock 'n' roll as being something that was very much to do with ordinary people in ordinary situations. 'The poetry of expression,' as it were. If he hadn't come along and suggest that we incorporate those images I think The Who would still have been a big band, but we'd probably have lived more in the shadow of the Stones than we have done."

His next job was to sell the concept to the media. With their hair freshly cut and blow-dried he had them photographed hanging around Piccadilly Circus by Eve Bowen – Entwistle, Moon and Townsend in nylon cycling jackets, Moon and Townshend in blue jeans with one-inch cuffs, Townsend in boxing boots, Daltrey in a white jacket and thin black tie. A four-

Opposite: The cover of Peter Meaden's four-page promotional brochure that drew attention to the hipness and mod authenticity of The High Numbers

page brochure fronted by a photo of a pensive Roger Daltrey in the white jacket boasted that the new single 'I'm The Face' was 'the first authentic mod record.'

Inside was Peter's advertising hype. "The important thing about the HIGH NUMBERS, which is immediately noted on meeting them, is that nothing is contrived or prefabricated about them and this can be said particularly in the field of clothes.

"The clothes they wear have the hallmark of the much maligned 'mod' – cycling jackets, tee shirts, turned up Levi jeans, long white jackets, boxing boots, black and white brogues and all the rest. But these are also worn by thousands of other young people of today. The Number, the Face, the Ticket, or to use a generalization, the Mod, is a product of this day and age. They can be seen in force, particularly any Saturday night in the clubs and on the streets of London's West End, and in nearly every large city in Great Britain.

"It is a way of life for them, an exciting way of life. And the fact that the HIGH NUMBERS are drawn from this facet of society in which they are totally immersed makes them about the most potentially exciting and powerful group in the field of beat music today. The things expressed on this, their first record, cause an immediate rapport between them and thousands of young people like themselves.

"In a nutshell – they are of the people."

Of course, The High Numbers couldn't have been more contrived in that they had been given their clothes, haircuts, name and debut songs, but they soon latched onto the mod scene and found ample sustenance for their music and developing image. The music papers and teenage girl magazines lapped up Peter's hyperbolic prose, uncritically buying into the image he was selling because it served them well and seemed to be so much of the moment. No one wanted to be left behind. "How mod are this mod-mad mob?" asked Peter Jones in *Record Mirror*

Opposite: The High Numbers in Meaden-issue mod gear: cycling jackets for Moon and Entwistle, two-tone brogues for Daltrey, and a giraffe-collared shirt for Townshend

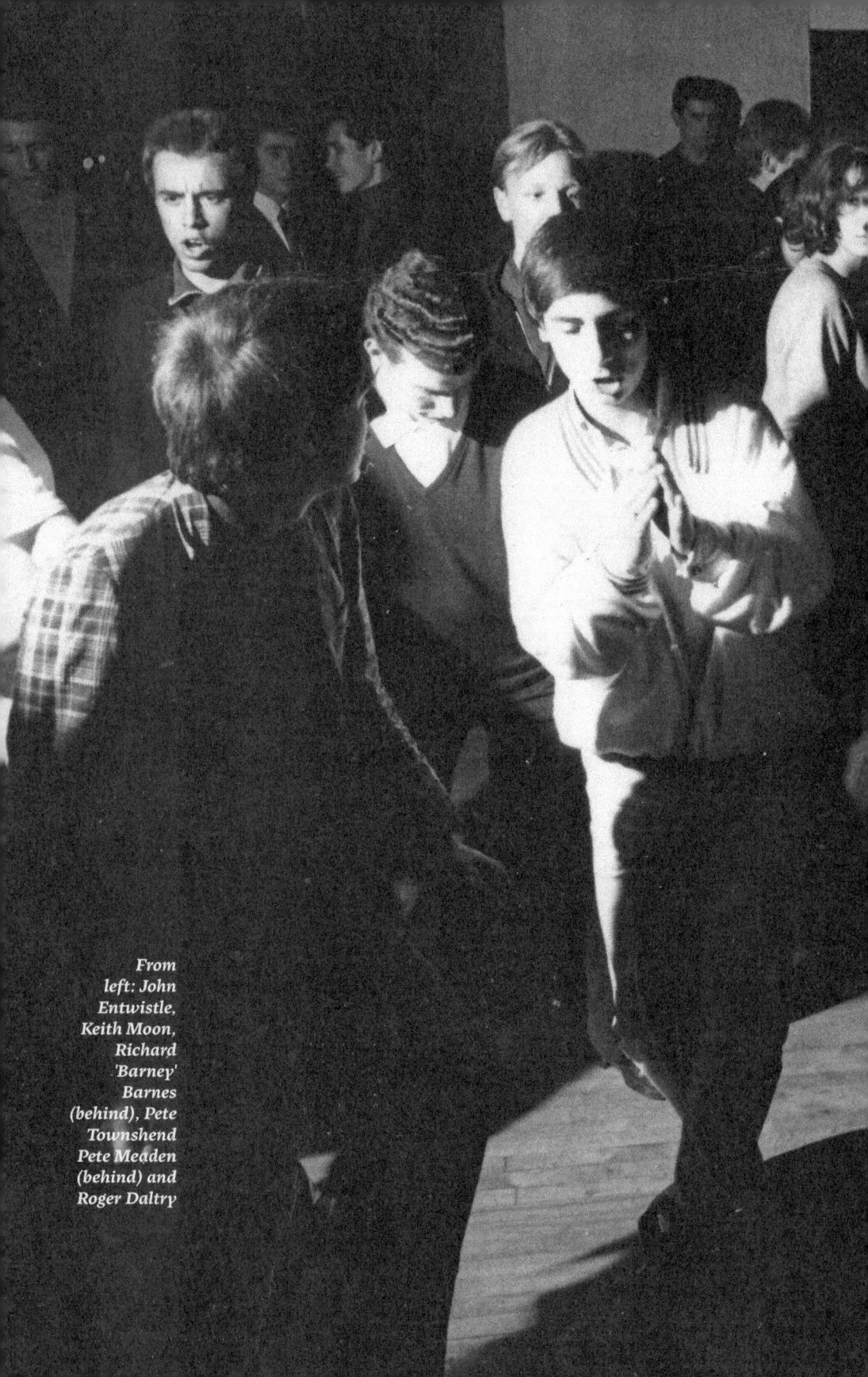

From left: John Entwistle, Keith Moon, Richard 'Barney' Barnes (behind), Pete Townshend Pete Meaden (behind) and Roger Daltry

on July 11. "VERY mod" he replied to himself. Roger spoke of how he dug the blues and Buddy Guy. Pete Townshend said he "spent a fortune on bright and in-vogue clothes" while Keith Moon confessed to spending "all my free time listening to the music in various West End clubs."

Further mod v rocker battles in Margate, Broadstairs, Brighton, Southend, Hastings and Bournemouth over the Whitsun holiday weekend in May had meant that even more media attention was being focused on the mod phenomenon. Rockers had been around for some time and their uniform was basic and settled. Mods, on the other hand, were new and more indicative of social changes likely to impact on the rest of the decade. Journalists were intrigued by them and wanted to know about their music tastes, drug consumption, sexual behaviour and patterns of spending.

Peter himself was profiled in the weekly girl's magazine *Boyfriend* as an eligible, and extremely hip, bachelor who liked girls with straight black or blonde hair and "tons of eye make-up." He was pictured wearing dark glasses, cropped hair and a check jacket. Already he was creating his own mythology. He took a year off his age, added an inch to his height and deftly produced two A level GCEs that he hadn't even studied for. His four-month stint abroad was stretched to seven months and included North Africa as well as Spain. He mentioned returning to England and immediately going off to America, a country he didn't visit until the mid-Seventies.

The piece was written in July 1964, just as 'I'm The Face' was released, and mentioned his past work handling publicity for The Crystals, Gene Pitney, the Stones and Georgie Fame, and his present managing The High Numbers and The Moments. It said that he also did publicity for Chuck Berry.

"He was the epitome of the speedfreak at the time," remembers Keith Altham, then a journalist with the teen magazine *Fabulous*. "He was shoveling amphetamines down

Opposite: Peter's profile in the girl's magazine Boyfriend portrayed him as hip and eligible and exaggerated everything from his height and school qualifications to his travel experience

82

Auburn-haired and blue-eyed, Peter's just a fraction under 6 ft. H was at grammar school and then he left for art school with five 'O levels and two 'A's to his credit. Art school lasted about one yea Later, Peter had left both school and home for a flat in Hampstead an a job in an advertising agency.

After that—another agency. Then he joined up with Andrew Oldha (the Stones' manager) to form an advertising agency, until last yea when he left the country for seven months. After making some mone in Spain and North Africa—'something to do with cars'—Peter arrive back in England and almost immediately flew off for a vacation America for three weeks. He gets around, this boy!

Back from the States, Peter tried his hand as a free-lance phote grapher and journalist for a while, then finally joined up again with hi old partner Andrew Oldham, handling publicity for the Crystals, Gen Pitney and the Stones.

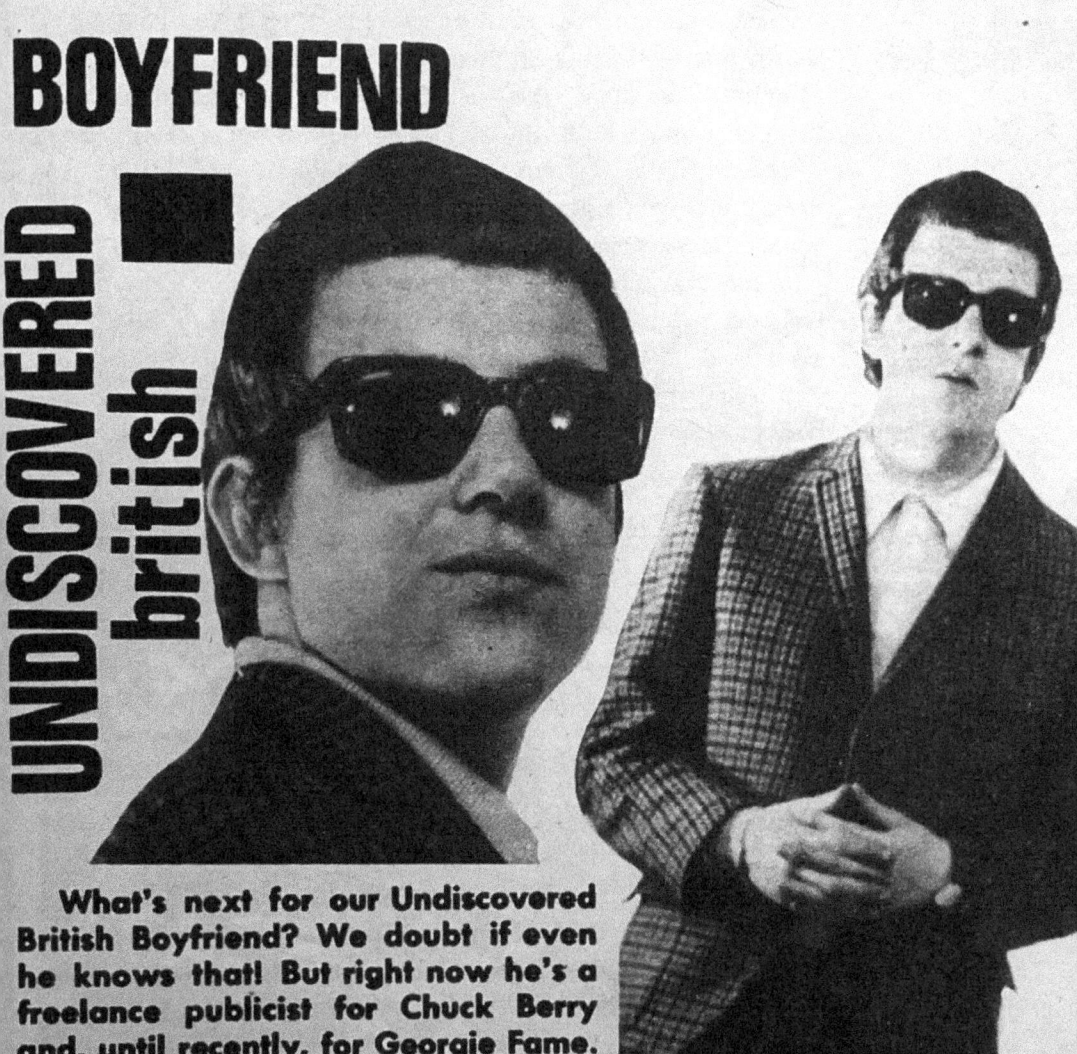

BOYFRIEND

UNDISCOVERED british

What's next for our Undiscovered British Boyfriend? We doubt if even he knows that! But right now he's a freelance publicist for Chuck Berry and, until recently, for Georgie Fame. On top of that he manages two

his throat. Consequently, what he had had to be taken with a pinch of salt. He certainly worked hard as a publicist. He came in raving about The High Numbers and had tremendous energy and enthusiasm. That was the good bit about him.

"We ran a photo of The High Numbers. June Southworth, who worked with me at the time, was very good at picking up on new bands. She was single whereas I was married so she got out a bit more than I did. She raved about them after she went to see them and her enthusiasm piqued my curiosity."

Southworth already knew Peter and she had been taken by Oldham to see the Stones at the Crawdaddy Club in May 1963, shortly after he'd first seen them. "He told me that they were so ugly I'd love them," she remembers. Peter, she thought at the time, was like A. A. Milne's Tigger. "He was full of energy and ideas. He had fluttering hands and a butterfly mind. His theatricality would put some people off. They wanted to un-bounce Tigger, but they never could."

He took her to see The High Numbers at the Bruce Grove Ballroom in Tottenham, a venue that turned out to be a rocker stronghold. "Roger was wearing his zoot suit jacket and Keith was in something garish and striped and they were surrounded by boys in leather looking very menacing,' she says. "A scuffle broke out and the group made a quick exit. When they got outside the mob caught up with them and Roger got pinned to the ground. Keith stood their laughing. Peter and John had bolted. Then I heard Peter pleading with these rockers saying, 'Do anything you like but don't touch the vocal chords.' It was hilarious!"

July 1964 proved to be Peter's peak moment. Everything at last seemed to be coming together. On July 6, the night that the film *A Hard Day's Night* premiered in London, he went to the 18th birthday party of Caroline Maudling, daughter of then Chancellor of the Exchequer Reginald Maudling. It was held at 11 Downing Street and made the next day's newspapers because Mick Jagger and Keith Richards were in attendance and Mike D'Abo's group A Band of Angels were the hired entertainment. Caroline was dating Scene Club owner Ronan O'Rahilly, who had recently launched Britain's first Pirate radio ship Radio Caroline (not named after her, but after the daughter of President Kennedy) and Peter was there with bass guitarist John Paul Jones, later to form Led Zeppelin with Robert Plant, John Bonham and Jimmy Page.

Here he met 19-year old Wendy Young, an art student who was living with The Pretty Things at 13 Chester Street, Belgravia and working as their housekeeper and general factotum. They took a liking to each other and began dating.

On July 22 The High Numbers began a three-month Wednesday night residency at The Scene club where they came face-to-face (as it were) with the hardcore mod audience that Peter had groomed them to appeal to. They were now playing some of Peter's favourite songs from Guy Stevens' collection including 'Long Tall Shorty' by Tommy Tucker (written by Don Covay), 'I Gotta Dance to Keep from Crying' by The Miracles and 'Pretty Thing' by Bo Diddley.

Allen Ellett of The Moments added keyboards on some numbers. "The kind of people they were playing to were mainly there to dance," he remembers. "They were there in their gear and they each wanted to be seen as the hippest person of the times. The reception for The High Numbers was good though. I never knew them to get a bad reception and I went on to play with them at places like the Goldhawk Club, the Railway Hotel at Harrow and Wealdstone and the Brighton Hippodrome."

In the sleeve notes for *Quadrophenia*, written in the voice of the album' tragic hero Jimmy, Pete Townshend offered up his view of what The High Numbers/Who became. "They were a mod group," he has Jimmy say. "Well, mods liked them. They weren't exactly mods, but mods did like them."

In 1968 Townshend explained the mods to *Rolling Stone*; "It was a movement of young people, much bigger than the hippie thing, the underground and all these things. It was an army, a powerful, aggressive army of teenagers with transport. Man, with these scooters and with their own way of dressing. It was acceptable, this was important; their way of dressing was hip, it was fashionable, it was clean and it was groovy.

"To be a mod you had to have short hair, money enough to buy a real smart suit, good shoes, good shirts; you had to be able to dance like a madman. You had to be in possession of plenty of pills all the time and always be pilled up. The groups that you liked when you were a mod were The Who. That's the story of why I dig the mods, man, because we were mods and that's how we happened. That's my generation – that's how the song 'My Generation' happened, because of the mods."

But July 1964 was also the beginning of the fall. It was the month that Kit Lambert first encountered the group at the Railway Hotel while he and his business partner Chris Stamp were idly looking for a group to build a film around. The couple began filming performances and by August was making approaches to sign the group to a management deal with their company New Action.

There are various versions of how Peter was ousted from his position, but his version is that Lambert approached him by saying he was a promoter interested in booking The High Numbers and Peter sold them to him in his usual manner as being the hippest, most happening group in London. This was music to the ears of Lambert who then spoke to Roger and Pete offering a lucrative deal with a guaranteed income. It's not hard to see the appeal. Peter, in his own words was 'fragile' and needed to be 'looked after' whereas Stamp and Lambert were both confident men with good connections. Stamp was a tough East Ender and the brother of trending actor Terence Stamp. Lambert came from the opposite end of the social spectrum and was the son of classical composer Sir Constance Lambert.

Opposite: Peter went to the 18th birthday party of Caroline Maudling, daugter of then Chancellor of the Exchequer Reginald Maudling, at 11 Downing Street

It's unlikely that there was ever a written contract between Peter and the group either as a manager or as a publicist. Their actual manager was Helmut Gorden, in partnership with booking agent Bob Druce whose USP was that he controlled several important pub and club venues in West London. However, Gorden had no real knowledge of the music business – he ran a firm that manufactured brass doorknobs – and so Peter was his man on the spot who accompanied the group to gigs and was paid to be their image-maker and link with the press.

According to Peter, Kit Lambert took him out for a meal at the Number Four Restaurant in Frith Street where he asked him to come up with a figure for severance pay. This was surely an honourable gesture rather than a legal obligation. Pete and Roger had probably asked Kit to make sure that Peter was looked after. He suggested a fee of £500 – a tidy sum in 1964 – and Peter agreed to it.

On August 2 Peter travelled down to Brighton to see The High Numbers appear at an 'All Nite Rave' at the Florida Room at Brighton Aquarium and found himself unable to get in. Despite his protestations that he knew the band, had written their current single and had done all their publicity to date he wasn't allowed entry. It was a huge blow to his self-esteem and one from which he never really recovered. In his mind the group were his mates and The High Numbers an accumulation of his dream for the mod movement and now he had been relegated to a position below that of a 'ticket'.

"We used to make sure that if there was a riot, a mod-rocker riot, we would be playing in the area," Townshend told *Rolling Stone*. "They used to assemble in Brighton. We'd always be playing there. And we got associated with the whole thing and got into the spirit of the whole thing...The music would come from the actual drive of the youth combination itself."

The High Numbers would go from strength to strength. In

Opposite: Chris Stamp (brother of actor Terence Stamp) and Kit Lambert (son of composer Constant Lambert) on the steps of Ronan O'Rahilly's offices in 6 Chesterfield Gardens, Mayfair, home of Radio Caroline

November they reverted back to calling themselves The Who and took up a Tuesday night residency at the Marquee Club in Wardour Street. The mod image cultivated by Peter was gradually adapted to incorporate fresh imagery – medals, targets, uniform jackets – inspired by Peter Townshend's knowledge of the emerging British pop art movement spearheaded by people like Peter Blake and Richard Hamilton. Their first single as The Who, 'I Can't Explain', saw them developing a jerky but explosive sound that was the perfect musical counterpart to the inarticulacy of the song's narrator.

They still appeared to be very much a mod group but were now leading rather than following. The fresh intake of mods with their Lambrettas and parka coats would soon be featuring symbols like the RAF roundel and the arrow from street signs on their clothing. Pete Townshend, who had befriended several mods from The Scene club and the Goldhawk Club in Shepherd's Bush, was listening to their dreams and anxieties and writing songs that put them into words and musical emotions. 'I'm The Face' and 'Zoot Suit' had only glossed the surface of the mod mind-set. 'I Can't Explain' went deeper into the heart of what it actually felt like to be both arrogant and uncertain at the same time.

Although 'Anyway Anyhow Anywhere' was Townshend's reflection on the life and musical style of Charlie Parker, it again touched on the search for liberation implicit in the mod experience. 'My Generation', released on October 29, 1965, was the ultimate summation of teenage restlessness, anger and desire for change. Peter had described mod as being 'anti family' meaning that it was anti settling down, adult responsibility and dull routine and 'My Generation' articulated exactly that with music that would be upsetting to anyone had settled down. It was noisy, frantic and discomforting. Roger's stuttered vocals suggested either restrained anger (was he about to utter the f-f-f-word?) or a blocked-up mind. "Peter thought we could pick

Opposite: The Who back on home turf in Shepherd's Bush, 1964. It was in this West London area that they first attracted a mod following

91

The Who on stage at The Marquee in Wardour Street, Soho. From November 24 1964 they played their brand of 'Maximum R&B' there every Tuesday until April 27, 1965

up on the mod thing and he was very right because mods had no focal point at all and The Who became that. We became the spokesmen," Roger Daltrey told me. "When Kit and Chris took over our management, they basically just took his ideas and made them bigger."

Peter didn't lose his vision for a group that would represent the mod experience but early in 1965, having lost The Who, he devoted the same energy to Jimmy James and The Vagabonds, a Jamaican group he found playing at the Overseas Visitors' Club in Earls Court. Whereas The High Numbers had been the sort of people mods might aspire to be, Jimmy James offered the soulful black club experience closer to that offered by American groups like The Impressions. They'd come to England in May 1964 playing calypso numbers for largely West Indian audiences in community halls, but their passion was for the American soul music that they'd heard on the radio in Jamaica.

"He came up and introduced himself," says James. "He was a real mod. He was the King of the Mods! He said he liked our sound and had a contact at the publishing house Jewel Music [Sandy Roberton] who at the time was getting a lot of stuff sent over from America for British bands to record. He said he could get us some stuff, and he did.

"What he liked about us was the composition of the band. There was nothing like it in Britain at the time. At the time you were dealing with white four-piece pop groups. We were black guys and we had a horn section and all this sort of thing. We seemed so different to him."

He introduced the group to Harold Pendleton of the Marquee and managed to get them a support spot with the Mike Cotton Sound in March 1965 that led regular bill topping shows starting in May. He found them gigs abroad in France, Belgium and Hungary. In June 1965 he wrote to his parents from Ostend; "Weather and hotel great. Food terrific. They've never seen anything like the Vagabonds here and the club goes wild every night. We are by far the biggest attraction in Ostend." In January 1966 he wrote from Budapest; "Happy New Year. We are having a great time. The only problem is how to spend our money. It is non-exchangeable into pounds. We live in the top hotel in Budapest and are treated like royalty." In June 1966 he was back in Ostend. "We are having a great time and fantastic receptions i.e. played the Moody Blues off the stage at a festival last night."

He composed the copy for the back cover of their debut album *The New Religion* and designed the layout with photos by Ivan Keeman. Even though this was pre-*Sgt. Pepper* he wanted the music to be orchestrated as an experience - the first seven songs for uplift, dancing and energy; the second seven songs for reflection, crashing out and coming down. "The two decks on this album have been carefully planned," he wrote, "and the tracks on each chosen, arranged and performed to complement two separate states of mind..." Side one was "a collection of pure distilled hip-swinging, toe-tapping, hand-clapping Rock 'n Roll soul." Side two was: "the most beautiful songs in the realm of Rhythm and Blues served a la New Wave."

His prose was reminiscent of his enthusiastic writing about the High Number – a mixture of hip slang and Old Testament prophecy. "AND SOMEWHERE IN THE MIDDLE IT CAME TO PASS that Count Prince Miller would shout to the faces: 'Wherever Jimmy James and The Vagabonds play, everyone and I mean everyone, is invited to a party. Forget you're in a club, it's Vag's party time and everybody knows everybody. So join in...let yourselves go...have fun!' And the faces would dig the rapport, jump on stage and have a ball. They would have TOTAL ENTERTAINMENT. And that's what it's all about.

"BUT – IN THE BEGINNING there was some two years back an exceptionally broke, eight-handed coloured band who played Rock 'n' Roll Soul and that not many people wanted to know (on account of no-one ever hearing of an English-based coloured band before and anyway groups were in that week) and this rather cheesed off and very hungry band drove, in their borrowed van, with half of The Who's equipment in the back (they dug this band) through the lower reaches of Hampshire on their way to their second date at The Birdcage Club in Portsmouth. They swung down that hill into Portsmouth. And there – lo and behold! Everywhere! Everywhere one could be stuck, were posters, posters and more posters. And feasting on them, this band read: THE NEW RELIGION JIMMY JAMES AND THE VAGABONDS – THERE AIN'T NO ONE ELSE! And they were nourished. Hence the title of this album. And from that moment in time on there has been no stopping the fantastic, exciting JIMMY JAMES AND THE VAGABONDS.

"Also in the beginning Jimmy James and Count Prince Miller, the rest of the Vags and myself met and found we shared a taste in a style of music that had never really been exposed in this country, except to a minority and then only on record in clubs such as The Scene and a few others around the country. Sure, people had heard records by Major Lance, Curtis Mayfield and The Impressions and more obscure items by William Bell, The Dells, Tony Clarke and a host of others. Products of big and small studios in the States, featuring huge, but at all times subtle, orchestras and choral units with unusual phrasing and clever arrangements but all with one thing in common – they were all basically Rock 'n' Roll. Updated certainly; more polished than raw unsophisticated R&B, but nevertheless carrying the same excitement; a form of music that had broadened the scope of Rock 'n' Roll and R & B and at the same time, encompassed them both. People had heard a few of these records but never enough to sell more than a first pressing. Pity. To our minds, it was, and is, the most exciting, melodically attractive and intelligent branch of pop. We were later to find the *Record Mirror's* Norman Jopling, also a long-time admirer of the work of The Impressions, had already given this music its perfect title; NEW WAVE RHYTHM AND BLUES. And this LP is our own New Wave R & B tribute to

Opposite: Jimmy James (second left) with Vagabonds Phil Chen (left, bass), Carl Griffiths (tenor sax) and Count Prince Miller (right, vocals)

Curtis Mayfield and his arranger Johnny Pate, for in popdom, no other team has contributed more.

"*And they made A Testament of Their Faith (henceforth to be known as this LP). On stage the Jimmy James and The Vagabonds Show works out like this: Jimmy (lead vocal), Count Prince Miller (compere, cheerleader and co-vocalist), Phillip Chen (bass), Wallace Wilson (vocals an lead guitar), Rupert Balgobin (drums), Carl Noel (organ), Matt Fredericks (tenor sax), Milton James (baritone sax). This is about as large a band as one can work with on the road but with it The Vags have achieved the enviable reputation of being the most exciting outfit in this country with their formula of power-packed Rock 'n' Roll played in all gears with aviation sound busting through on both carbs. But record-wise we have the need to broaden out. We have attempted here in fourteen tracks and with nearly £2000 spent on production alone, to present the most enjoyably comprehensive Pop-Rock-Soul anthology ever made, and it is all within the framework of New Wave R&B. Our first obligation is to our friends in the clubs who pay to see us, jump on stage and have a ball and never see us dragging up in sports cars because we have done all our bread in on this LP... A few of the numbers here you will have heard performed live on stage – but not like this. With the use of a 50 piece orchestra and such names as Doris Troy, Madeleine Bell and Goldie helping out on vocals I Give You A Study In Progressive Pop By Jimmy James And The Vagabonds.*

Peter Meaden"

Opposite: Major Lance was one of the black artists whose music appealed to Peter and The Scene club regulars. His Okeh single 'The Monkey Time' was a particular favourite

Jimmy James was now playing Peter's idea of perfect pop. The majority of the album's tracks were from singles that had become Scene Club hits – Tony Clarke's 'Ain't Love Good, Ain't Love Proud', The Miracles' 'I Gotta Dance to Keep From Crying', Gene Chandler's 'I'm Just A Fool For You Girl', The Radiants' 'It Ain't No Big Thing' and The Impressions' 'People Get Ready'. Norman Jopling, who he credited in the sleeve notes, was a Scene Club habitué and a *Record Mirror* writer responsible for championing R&B in the UK. He would become a close friend, flat mate and later a business partner of Peter's.

"Peter was influential on our music in that he came up with new songs from publishers for us to record and he was influential on our style – the way we dressed," says James. "When we arrived from Jamaica we wore band uniforms with collarless jackets. He took us to Lord John in Carnaby Street where we had suits made for us and started buying buttoned down collar shirts and slim ties."

His plan worked. For the second time he had a band receptive to his ideas who he was able to market to the mod audience. In the publicity kit sent to journalists was a four-page explanation entitled Social Significance. Key to this was the idea that 'they stand for the mod generation.' The piece went on; "This cult of excitement-seeking youngsters has stood by and followed The Vagabonds since they made their first appearance at the Scene... The group's name is virtually a password for this with-it crowd of girls and boys. The Vags certainly don't mind being tied to one particular cult as these fellas and gals have done so much for the group. Besides this, there is the fact now that the mod generation having multiplies over the past three years these kids are so powerful now that they can dictate what's 'coming in' and what's 'going out' both disc-wise and clothes-wise.'

Jimmy James and The Vagabonds became hugely popular in mod-oriented clubs around the country. "We were the only band in the country playing that type of stuff until Geno Washington and The Ram Jam Band came along."

But by the time New Religion was released, in December 1966, the mod scene was waning. The Scene club had closed earlier in the year after repeated raids by the Drug Squad finally resulting in manager Lionel Blake being sentenced (in January 1966) to a year's imprisonment for "keeping a disorderly house," the pirate radio ships were being threatened by legislation that would make their broadcasts illegal, Ready Steady Go! made its last transmission on December 23 and many of the key mod figures had moved on. Mickey Tenner went to Spain to work as a DJ, Phil The Greek was now a senior stylist with Vidal Sassoon, Guy Stevens had become a record producer, other mods were marrying and moving out of London. The trend in music was away from dance music and towards screwier more cerebral sounds. Bob Dylan had released *Blonde on Blonde* in May 1966, The Beatles released *Revolver* in August and the latest singles by The Who were 'Happy Jack' and 'Pictures of Lily'.

The London club scene was also changing as the audience matured. There was a renewed emphasis on dining, decor and comfort. Sybilla's opened in Swallow Street in June 1966, The Bag o' Nails in Kingley Street in November, and in December came The Speakeasy in Margaret Street and boxer Billy Walker's Uppercut Club in Forest Gate. The Roundhouse in Camden began to be used as a venue for the heavier rock bands and the psychedelic club UFO opened in Tottenham Court Road in December. "People moved on," observes Lionel Blake. "More sophisticated clubs opened up. People lost interest. Peter lost interest."

On May 30, 1967 Peter married Wendy Young, his girlfriend of the past three years, at Islington Register Office. "It wasn't a big wedding, says Gerald Meaden. "It was what Wendy and everybody else wanted. I don't think she meant all that much to him. Wendy was brainy. She was very clever. She knew everything that was going on. Because she was from the north, from Sheffield, she wasn't soft and silly like a lot of the rich girls down in London."

Mod, as a subculture committed to movement, perpetual change and being ahead of the crowd, necessarily contained the seeds of its own destruction. Programmes like *Ready, Steady, Go!* promoted the new dances, music and looks to a national audience and so it became ever more urgent to keep adapting in order to maintain that aura of being special. But also, by transmitting images of the latest London mod styles to the whole nation it dimished their exclusivity. Teenagers in Dumfries, Llandudno, Coleraine and Truro could now quickly copy these fashions.

Another significant factor in the destruction of mod was the spread of LSD. Drinamyl encouraged a lot of body action and fast-talking but LSD and other hallucinogenics such as mescaline and peyote produced reflection, introversion and a laid-back lifestyle. The inner life became more important than outer activities. The appropriate music orchestrated good trips or, for those not tripping, mimicked the disotortions and time shifts. Clothing fabrics changed from tonik and seersucker to satin and velvet, patterns from checks and stripes to paisley, haircuts from razorcuts to anything wild and long, jeans from straight legged Levis to bellbottoms and loon pants.

Pete Townshend took his first LSD trip on a plane to America to perform at the Monterey Festival in June 1967 – the world's first large-scale open-air rock event and a precursor to Woodstock. He'd taken it to join Keith Moon and prevent him from feeling alone on the flight, but it resulted in what he called "the most disturbing experience I've ever had." He felt that he'd left his body and had floated to the ceiling. Moon brought his stash of pure Owsley LSD to the Speakeasy in Margaret Street, London, on July 13 and gave (or sold) some to Peter who shared it the next day with his old mod friend Norman Jopling. It was Peter's second trip but Jopling's first. Jopling later wrote; "It was the full-blown born-again beyond-the-white-light experience and the visual effects stayed with me for the next three weeks. I was changed. When I came back to earth next morning, renewed, I felt like I'd landed on another Earth in a parallel universe – which is where I've been ever since."

Opposite: Peter's future wife, Wendy Young, with Dick Taylor (left) and John Stax (right) of The Pretty Things on the front steps of the band's upmarket Belgravia home

Peter isn't on record describing his initial experience of LSD but what's certain is that the drug interfered with his already delicate and highly imaginative mind and sent him on a downward spiral. He must have liked it because he took it

repeatedly, but it slowly warped his sense of reality.

For some people LSD opened up a world of vibrant colour, beautiful sounds and feelings of warmth towards humanity. For others it was like taking the lid off a snake pit. Peter was one of the others. He called himself the Black Tripper and disassociated himself from those who wore bells around their necks and flowers in their hair.

The same year he also stopped working with Jimmy James and The Vagabonds. There are various explanations as to why this happened. Gerald Meaden says it was because James disapproved of his irresponsible use of drugs. James says it was because Peter misappropriated the band's funds and bought himself a mini car (despite being unable to drive). John Emery, who was hired as the group's publicist, thinks it was because James had been urged by others to consider making a go of a solo career.

"They were going out for £800 a night in 1967 and that was fantastic money at the time," explains Emery. "They also had a fabulous deal with Pye. Then, according to Peter, the money was coming in so thick and fast they had to hire an accountant who persuaded Jimmy that he was better off on his own. Peter suddenly found that all the cheques he'd used to pay for utilities out of the band's account had bounced. The accountant had taken over Jimmy's management."

In March or April of 1967 Peter had set up an independent production company called New Wave Records with his old mod pal and R&B expert Norman Jopling. The plan was to discover artists, find songs, produce records and release them through Polydor. In Manchester Peter scoured a club in Moss Side and found half a dozen young West Indians who he thought he could mould into the new Temptations. He named them The Alphabets and brought them down to London for a recording session only to find that the lead singer's vocal cords tensed up under pressure. When Peter tried to cajole him to try harder the man produced a knife. The dream of a Motown-like sensation from the North ended right there.

Another boy he'd found during the same trip at least made a record. He was named Ossie and Peter put him in the studio with a group of session musicians he called The Sweet Boys. Ossie and The Sweet Boys recorded a cover of Toussaint McCall's 'Nothing Takes the Place of You' with an instrumental B side titled 'Brixton Boo-ga-loo' and it became the first New Wave Productions release on Polydor. Peter produced an image for Ossie that was somewhere between James Brown and Little Richard – a tangerine suit, a chauffeur with silk handkerchiefs to mop his brow and, according to the press release, "a fly swatter to keep away over enthusiastic admirers, most of whom want to touch the hem of Ossie's garments." After the failure of the single (released in June 1967), and the disinterest of the hip cognoscenti at the Speakeasy where he played one night, Ossie just disappeared. His follow-up single was recorded but never released.

Norman Jopling placed an advert in *Record Mirror's* classified section: "WANTED – Folk, or folk rock, male group or solo artist for management and recording. Replies box 0078." Among the responses was one that particularly stood out. It came from four musicians who had met at Wolverhampton Art College and had produced an acetate recording of their songs. They were Stephen Morris, Dave Cartwright, Patrick Burston and Stephen Stringer. Jopling named them The Peep Show.

They were unlike anything that had appealed to them before. The music of The Peep Show was gentle, reflective and ornate. It had none of the pumping dance rhythms of records by Stax, Motown and Sue. Even though at this point none of the group members had taken the drug they were in tune with the new introspective movement. Over the coming months they recorded a single 'Your Servant Stephen' backed with 'Mazy,' a track that would go on to be regarded as a classic of British psychedelia.

Peter was now a total convert to acid and its transformative properties. In October 1967 he saw an import copy of the recently released album *Safe as Milk* by Captain Beefheart and His Magic Band in the window of One-Stop Records in South Moulton Street and, intrigued by the cover, bought it. The music he heard led him to believe he'd met a brother in madness and from that moment on he made it his mission to get Captain Beefheart to Britain and to ensure that *Safe as Milk* got a UK release.

Don Van Vliet, then 25 years old, was a musician, songwriter and visual artist from California who described his records to one interviewer as "music to dematerialize the catatonia." His songs were quite unlike anything most pop music lovers had ever heard. His voice was discordant, the structures and rhythms were unorthodox, and his lyrics ranged from the eccentric to the inexplicable.

During this time Peter was "developing the talent" (his phrase) of an informal band headed by Dave Brock that would later morph into Hawkwind. Brock's fellow guitar player Mick Slattery knew Peter and took Brock to his flat in Offord Road, Islington, to meet him. Slattery was impressed with his stereo sound system, the first of its kind that he'd ever encountered. Peter put on records by Sopwith Camel, The Electric Prunes, Country Joe & The Fish and Captain Beefheart while spiking their drinks with acid. Slattery had tripped before, but the experience still came as a complete shock. (Peter had previously spiked the drinks of the members of The Peep Show, causing one of the members to be temporarily hospitalized.)

Opposite: The Peep Show was the second signing to New Wave Productions, the company set up by Peter and Record Mirror journalist Norman Jopling

"He had all these arty books and [reproductions] of Turner paintings," Brock told Hawkwind biographer Carol Clerk. "I'd never take LSD before. It was put into sugar lumps using eyedroppers. He'd spiked me in a cup of tea! He said 'I don't want you getting into a panic. I've just dropped some LSD into your tea.' I had a wonderful trip."

More recently Brock told a journalist. "It was nice music to drop acid to. He also had some good books on art which I remember going through. When you looked at Turner's paintings on LSD it was a revelation. They were all moving. You could see spirits in the winds coming up with the ghost ship in the estuary." Shortly after this Peter took Slattery and Brock into the studio and had them record a wild version of Beefheart's album track 'Electricity.'

Another person Peter tried to convert to LSD was music publisher Sandy Roberton. He invited him over to his flat, gave him a dose and put a copy of *Sergeant Pepper's Lonely Hearts Club Band* on the stereo. "My wife came with me because she was worried that something terrible would happen to me and I'd end up with only half a brain," he says. "Peter told me it would blow my mind and it did actually. The staccato guitar on 'Getting Better' is unbelievable when you're on acid. Those guys made that record for people to enjoy when they were slightly out of it. It took a whole day for it to wear off. And I never did it again."

Under the aegis of New Wave Productions Peter set about bringing Captain Beefheart's Magic Band to London. He arranged dates for them but when the required work permits weren't forthcoming he didn't tell the band, hoping that everything would work out anyway. As a result, Beefheart and his band members were refused entry when they arrived at Heathrow in January 1968 and had to leave the country and return when the problem was sorted.

Opposite: Sleeve of Captain Beefhear's Safe as Milk which Peter saw in a record shop window. The music he heard led him to believe he'd found a brother in madness

The Immigration Department described Don Van Vliet as "the leader of an American 'pop' group known as Captain Beefheart's Magic Band, which specializes in so-called psychedelic music and is currently very popular with a certain section of the population of the West Coast of the United States." The Magic Band, the report went on "presented a very strange appearance, being attired in clothing ranging from 'jeans' to purple trousers, with shorts of various hues, and wearing headgear varying

from conical witches' hats to a brilliant yellow safety helmet of the type worm by construction engineers." When they were interviewed by immigration officials; "it proved somewhat difficult...as they appeared to think on a completely different mental plane..."

The report made by the immigration officials makes interesting reading. "At this stage a gentleman dressed in the American style, with long unkempt hair and with a cigarette dangling from his lower lip, approached the control and introduced himself as Mr. Peter Alexander Edwin Meaden, born 11. 11. 41, British, and described in his passport as an 'artistes' manager.' Mr. Meaden said that he represented New Wave Records Ltd, 17-19 Stratford Place, London, which firm was sponsoring the group's visit to the United Kingdom, in conjunction with the group's American recording company, Kama Sutra/ Buddha Records Ltd, New York."

Peter denied that the band was here to work, saying that they'd only flown in to talk to the press. As he had no business card and no proof that he represented the group the Special Branch was called to run a background check. They reported that he had previous convictions for illegal possession of a Sten gun, taking a motor vehicle that didn't belong to him and selling liquor without a license. Because of this, and despite his protestations, the officials "strongly suspected that the group was going to take engagements in this country." A copy of *NME* was found and, lo and behold, there was Captain Beefheart and his Magic Band advertised to appear at the Middle Earth club in Covent Garden and the Speakeasy in Margaret Street that weekend. "Faced with this Mr. Meaden at first protested his innocence but finally both he and the group admitted that the engagements had been arranged. Mr. Meaden then pleaded for clemency on the grounds of his own stupidity, a plea which was rejected."

The immigration department quickly worked out that Beefheart and his band were the innocent victims and Mr.

Opposite: Wendy, Peter and Sacha pictured in 1968 the year of his first mental breakdown. "They weren't really a very loving couple," said Peter Anders. "You didn't see them hugging."

Meaden was the source of the problem. They spent four hours on the 'phone speaking to the Home Office, the Ministry of Labour, Equity (the actors' union), Pye Records and even Artie Ripp of Kama Sutra Records in New York. Their eventual decision was that the musicians had to go on to Hanover in Germany from where they could re-enter Britain once the permits were sorted.

The Immigration Department's conclusion was; "Mr. Meaden, on whose shoulders the blame for all the whole incident must rest, was told by Mr. Ripp that his association with Kama Sutra ceased forthwith and he was a dejected man as he departed, muttering under his breath."

Incidents like this that undermined his confidence, plus the heavy use of LSD, appear to have tipped him over the edge. In July 1968 he had a severe breakdown and was taken to Claybury Hospital, a 'mental home' at Woodford Green, Essex. There he was diagnosed with paranoid schizophrenia and received 20 treatments of electroconvulsive therapy (ECT) that involved passing electric currents through his brain to produce brief seizures that were at the time believed to positively alter the brain chemistry. He was also prescribed the anti-psychotic drug Stelazine that he continued to take for the next five years.

This was the start of a period during which he worked only sporadically. In a press release where he wrote about himself in the third person in 1975 he explained it this way: "Late in 1968 Peter fell sick and was hospitalized. His doctors warned him to stay away from rock 'n' roll, so he spent the next two years convalescing." Says Gerald Meaden, "He'd been sharing a flat with Norman Jopling, but when he came home to us he was really strange. It was as if he had no vision and couldn't hear anything. He crashed out." His psychiatrist later concluded that his original mental condition might not have been schizophrenic but drug-induced. Peter admitted to the hospital that he had been taking LSD, Pethadine, amphetamines, cocaine, Dexedrine and barbiturates.

As the movement he most closely identified with, and the music he loved, receded into the past, he realised that he was no longer the Face, the King, the man on the cutting edge. The world he best understood was now a part of pop cultural history and the new world was not to his liking. Mod, he later told journalist Penny Valentine, was "a whole movement with its own uniforms and language, its own drugs like pills and Drinamyl – very up, speedy stuff, very outgoing. Then acid came along and (there was) a loss of identity. Now kids don't have it anymore. The only ones that can cut it these days are the spade kids." Those who live by the zeitgeist, die by the zeitgeist.

His projects now had little cohesion or sense of direction. He still had a reputation as "the man who discovered The Who" or "London's ace mod", and some artists still thought he might sprinkle some magic dust over their careers, but his choices now seemed to be governed more by happenstance and pressing financial need than any vision for cultural change or commitment to a particular subculture. As New Wave Productions he and Norman Jopling produced singles for the American soul singer Donnie Elbert who'd had regional success in the late Fifties and early Seventies, but they failed to revive his career.

He returned to the business in the autumn of 1970 to work with Tony Hall at Tony Hall Enterprises, mainly doing promotion on artists like The Real Thing and Arrival. Tony Hall Enterprises briefly managed a trio composed of American bass player Alan Merrill, Israeli guitarist Jake Hooker and British drummer Paul Varley. Peter named them Arrows as a tribute to The Who's famous symbol, had them rehearse at studios in Chelsea and constantly chipped in with suggestions not only for their image but for their music. "He was clearly a hands-on manager," says Merrill. "He wanted to create a clear-cut media image for each member of the band. He felt that this aspect was crucial for developing a successful act."

Desperate for an income, they began visiting publishing companies and playing their new songs. One company that showed exceptional interest was RAK whose publishing was run by Dave Most and record label by his brother Mickie. Mickie Most had a song – 'Touch Too Much' - and wanted to produce it as a single. He thought the Arrows might be the band to do the recording. Excitedly, the group went back to Peter with the news.

"He told us vehemently, with much physical animation, that it would be a mistake," remembers Merrill. "Waving his arms about he explained the drawbacks of signing with Mickie. 'He'll turn you into a teenybop act,' he said. He then said that if we signed with RAK he'd have to bow out of the picture. He said that he'd still support the band and would remain our friend, but he'd feel uncomfortable working with Mickie Most. It simply wouldn't work. He didn't elaborate," Arrows went with RAK and had three UK chart singles in 1974 and 1975 (all on RAK and produced by Mickie Most), two TV series called *Arrows* on Granada Television in 1976 and 1977 and one song, 'I Love Rock 'n' Roll,' that was covered by Joan Jett and the Runaways, managed by Kenny Laguna, and became a huge international hit. True to his word, Peter had bowed out before any of this happened

Opposite: Although the record executive Tony Hall irked Peter by referring to him as a 'pilled-up mod' in 1964, the two worked together in the Seveties to promote the likes of Arrival and The Real Thing

In 1973 Peter worked in an unofficial capacity with Motown's London production company that owned the labels Rare Earth and MoWest. At the request of A&R man Trevor Churchill he was brought in to look after their artists in an ill-defined way. "I thought I was the businessman and he could be the guy who got on with the artists," says Churchill. "It was as simple as that. I knew he wasn't terribly organised and had various drug problems, but he had flair. Sometimes the artists wouldn't go along with his ideas though. We had a group called Slowbone and Peter had all these ideas of how to change them, but these

guys were from the East End and wanted nothing to do with it."

He fared better with a trio of East Coast American producers, musicians and songwriters – Peter Anders, Paul Naumann and Kenny Laguna – who came to London hoping to bring some polish to the Motown stable. Churchill gave Peter the job of settling them in, familiarising them with London and sorting out their everyday needs. "Peter ran everything from sorting out lodgings, keeping my diary and making sure I got to places on time," says Anders. "I found him charming. I didn't know anyone who didn't like him. He pulled me in certain directions – like pointing me to people in London who were looking for new material. I got involved with Dave Edmunds and wrote some original music for the movie *Stardust*. Peter was very instrumental in that."

Anders, who was heavily involved with hard drugs, had what he refers to as "an indiscretion" with Wendy Meaden. "I'm not proud of it," he says. "Peter was a little disappointed, to put it mildly. He wasn't angry though. He knew that I would never have done anything like that if it hadn't been for the drugs. Peter wasn't crazy about women. Even when he was living with Wendy, they weren't really a very loving couple. You didn't see them hugging or stuff like that."

His lack of regular income and bouts of manic behaviour put additional strain on his already fragile marriage to Wendy. They had a son, Sacha Benedict Meaden (born 1968), and yet Peter had little sense of family responsibility. Domesticity didn't suit him. At one point he decided to strip himself of all belongings and so destroyed all his books, photographs, drawings, letters, documents and other possessions.

Opposite: Celebrated American producer Kenny Laguna with Peter during the recording of Rollin' On, *the successful 1977 album by The Steve Gibbons Band*

During this period he sought out his old friend Iain Sinclair who he'd first met in Guildford back in the Fifties. "You could see things gradually getting worse," says Sinclair. "He came to stay with me in Cambridge and was in a bit of a state without anywhere to live and his marriage broken up. We had kids and he was getting to be

a bit of a problem, so he then stayed with a friend of mine, Chris Curry, who was the guy who started Acorn Computers."

Curry didn't know much about mods or rock music and was the local candidate for the United Democratic Party, a right-wing fringe party that was "anti Common Market and followed the economics of Enoch Powell." This was during the rather grim period of strikes, power cuts and the three-day working week. There was a widespread feeling that Britain was in a severe decline and needed a good dose of old-fashioned law and order to bring it back to where it rightly belonged.

Peter was quite inspired by Curry's politics. It reignited his vision for organising armies of clean-living young people and his fascination with the acquisition and administration of power. "He never stopped telling us how he could, at a moment's notice, raise an army," says Curry. "He said that he had organised the mods in their thousands and was still capable of doing it. He had a great fascination with power. He said that you had to overwhelm people with your presence, and he had decided that the way to do this was to use obscenity casually in normal conversation.

"He then proceeded to do this. He would use the obscenest language without raising his voice. He would say it as if it was perfectly normal but just loud enough that other people around him could hear. His would happen in the local pubs and it would either result in customer complaints or the landlord would ask me never to bring him back. We got banned from at least three pubs where I had been a regular customer."

He was drinking heavily, and Curry suspected was also taking drugs. "He could be very bright and effective one minute but a bit of a ranting lunatic the next." In his disturbed mind he was about to make a comeback as a politician rather than the image-maker of a pop group. "People with strong personalities or strong driving forces can switch totally from one sphere of interest to another," remarks Curry. "We definitely caught him during his political and rather dangerous mode rather than his music promotion mode."

He moved into an apartment in Lambolle Road, Belsize Park, with Norman Jopling where on April 1st 1975 he caused such a disturbance that he had to be physically removed. "Peter picked up a tin of yellow paint and threw it over the walls," remembers Peter's friend, journalist John Emery. "Norman had to call in two doctors to have him sectioned on the spot. He was taken to a horrible hospital, Claybury, at Woodford Bridge in Essex. Wendy told me she could no longer deal with him. His mother told me the same thing." He was kept there until May 30 as he was judged by the psychiatrists to be "aggressive, irrational and 'hypomanic'."

This was immediately before I met him after tracking him down via the music publisher for 'I'm The Face'. He was excited to do the interviews not only because it involved talking about the highlights of his life to an interested party but also because it reconnected him with The Who.

Although The Who had never wronged Peter in any way, they were aware of the devastating effect on him that their break had caused and were happy to play a part in his rehabilitation. Peter's latest passion was for the Steve Gibbons Band, a straightforward rock 'n' roll act fronted by a singer of Birmingham Sixties beat group The Uglys and featuring the Move's founder and guitarist Trevor Burton. The Who's management company, Trinifold, gave Peter an office and allowed him to manage the band under their auspices.

Peter had first seen the Steve Gibbons Band at the Hope and Anchor in Upper Street, Islington, and later travelled to Birmingham to see one of their regular pub gigs. "I spotted him straight away," says Gibbons, "because he was sitting in the front of the room. He didn't look like any of the regular punters. He was transfixed throughout the set and, after it was over, came up and introduced himself. He was staying at the Albany Hotel and so me and the bass player went back with him and talked to us for about an hour and a half. What impressed me that all his talk was about what we'd played. There was nothing about business or deals."

He then brought Pete Townshend to see them and, finally, The

Who's manager Bill Curbishley. Both Burton and Gibbons were under contract to Tony Secunda, the man who had managed Burton's previous group The Move, so a meeting was arranged for all the involved parties where Curbishley asked Secunda what it would cost to release them, got out his cheque book and paid the requested amount.

Gibbons, who had thick dark hair and a beard and dressed in a Mississippi gambler's jacket, leather jeans and boots, was a charismatic performer and wrote music that was hard to classify. Some of it was straight out of the Eddie Cochran or Chuck Berry songbook but he had a Dylanesque delight in language and phrasing and experimented with tracks that sounded as if they could have been written by Raymond Chandler and delivered by Jack Kerouac. He was simultaneously in love with the past and imagining the future. Peter later told Dave Laing of *Sounds*; "It blew my mind. It was the most exciting thing I'd seen for five years. It gave me those rock and roll tingles and I wanted to get involved."

As with The Who and Jimmy James and The Vagabonds, Peter had strong ideas about the way they should look and what image they should cultivate. "Some of his ideas were outrageous," says Gibbons. "He wanted me to look like some Doc Holliday character and I went along with that – I was already wearing knee-length boots and waistcoats – but he wanted me in jodhpurs. That was a dangerous area – black boots and jodhpurs! It was reminiscent of the Iron Dream book that he constantly spoke about. From the word go he spoke about the way people looked. Nearly everyone wore denim during that period, but he hated it and so did I."

For the first time in years Peter had a regular income, a responsible position, a degree of influence and a workplace to go to. He thrived in the new environment, working out of offices on Wardour Street alongside Bill and Jackie Curbishley, receptionist Caroline Guinness and management assistant Chris Chappel, with regular visits from members of The Who's crew such as sound engineers Bob Pridden and Cy Langston and production manager John 'Wiggy' Wolff. The

Opposite: Peter developed an image for Steve Gibbons based on the 19th century gambler and gunfighter Doc Holliday. "Nearly everyone wore denim in that period," says Gibbons. "But Peter hated it. And so did I."

Steve Gibbons Band became support act to The Who and this took Peter out on the road in Britain, Europe and America during 1976.

During this period his mother apparently broke the news to him that Stanley Meaden was not his biological father and that he was the result of wartime romance with a Canadian airman. Unusually she chose to reveal this to Peter in a letter sent to Trinifold. "He had recently had an argument with her," recalls Jackie Curbishley. "I remember very well that there had been a fight and he was staying with someone else. She sent him various mementoes of his father – maybe a dog tag or a military record book. That was when he realized he could possibly track him down."

Initially he was elated by the idea that he was not genetically tied to a staid furniture polisher from North London but to a Canadian serviceman. He imagined the leather helmets, the goggles and the fur lined boots. He imagined him dodging flak over enemy territory and the plane dropping its payload. Like Andrew Loog Oldham, he now had transatlantic connections. "He was really proud of that," Gibbons recalls. "He mentioned it frequently."

He managed to trace his birth father's location, but no one is sure whether he discovered what had happened to him by postal enquiry or whether, while in Toronto on tour with Steve Gibbons, he went knocking on doors and was given the news by a widow. The conclusion, however, is in no doubt. Peter discovered that his mother's former lover had died two years previously. They would never be reconciled. He would never discover how much of his character or his talent had been inherited from this man. "When he found out that his father had died it was a huge body blow to him," says Gibbons. "He had visions of getting to know him. I think the discovery had a strong bearing on the way his life mapped out after that."

His life then seemed to unravel at an even faster rate. He retreated further inside himself. "He became more insular after he found out about his father's death," says Jackie. "He never used to close his office door but after that he became very depressed about the whole

Opposite: Who manager, Bill Curbishley with Peter in the Seventies. Curbishley helped bring him back into the fold of The Who after a decade in the wilderness

situation and I did notice that he used to close his office door. I think it tipped the balance for him. He suddenly talked about it a lot."

Working at Trinifold he was privy to the development of the *Quadrophenia* film, based on The Who's 1973 release. So much of the album had resonated with him. It was, after all, about a young London mod with identity problems that considered himself to be a face. Once of the songs, 'Cut My Hair', even quoted from his High Numbers' lyric for 'I'm the Face'. There's no question that the album was inspired by the mod experience that Peter had opened up for the group in 1964 and Pete Townshend even gave him a cheque and a letter outlining his gratitude (which Peter had framed).

Director-writer Franc Roddam met with Peter during his visits to the office. "What I remember is this sense of myself as an interloper," he says. "He was a real mod and I was about to make a film about mods. This guy really knows his stuff. He really does have style. I should hang with him a bit. I was making a mod film, but I had other agendas too. So, I had this mod in front of me and I thought – I can learn from this guy.

"I remember showing him photos of the cast and talking to him about different tailors I did meet some old mods and they almost certainly came to me though him. In a way he was a pinnacle of modism, but he was intelligent too. I felt a strange obligation to live up his standard when it came to the mods. I paid a little more attention than I might otherwise have done if he hadn't been there. Had he lived, he would have been a bigger influence on the film than he was."

The sadness that now seemed to clothe him also struck Roddam. "I look at things from the point of view of a director and writer and I could see this beautifully turned out guy sitting in a small office surrounded by gold and platinum discs earned by The Who. I think that must have been torture for him. Everywhere he looked there was testament to his folly. It seemed to drain him of colour and drain him of life. It was just through that one move of selling the band. I thought it must be a further beating up for him to have this guy coming in who doesn't look like a mod who was going to do a film about mods."

Divorced from Wendy since 1975 (they had separated in 1973) he was now living back with his parents at Edmonton where he took up residence in the small upstairs back bedroom. His sexuality puzzled some people. While there was no evidence that he was gay he was almost never seen with a girlfriend. His attention to stylish detail, his fixation on male heroes and his partiality for the imagery of leather clad men might have implied that he was at least bi-sexual, but it was most likely no more than a mod fascination with masculine power and the sensual side of clothing.

He seemed to dislike intimacy with women – or, at least, the kind of intimacy that would necessitate becoming emotionally involved. He had a sneaking admiration for sex workers because they could give a man pleasure without demanding any responsibility. Maybe he was fearful of being drawn into the sort of loveless marriage he imagined most couples were condemned to in their thirties. Maybe he never felt the same degree of intensity in the companionship with women that he felt in his companionship with male mods and musicians.

Steve Gibbons recalls being on tour with him in Germany when Peter went off into the red light district and sampled the wares of a brothel. "I stood outside in the corridor waiting for him and I could hear all the goings on. I eventually went out on the street. He did like to have a walk on the wild side. But I think he thought that if was going to have sex at all he would do it with prostitutes. He almost had a slight dislike of women."

Chris Chappel remembers that he liked to occasionally treat himself with a visit to a massage parlour in Soho but also that he had a girlfriend of sorts while at Trinifold. "She was very glamorous and had an exotic name. She may even have been a stripper. He kept her very much to himself. I think she lived in Soho and she'd always arrive at the office after working hours. Given that people like Keith Moon were floating around I don't think he wanted to let anyone

else near her. He was very proprietary."

In August 1977 the Steve Gibbons Band had a Top Twenty hit in Britain with a cover version of the Chuck Berry song 'Tulane' that was recorded on the banks of the Thames at Pete Townshend's Eel Pie Studios in Twickenham. It came from the band's second album *Rollin' On*, for which Peter had managed to secure his old song writing friend Kenny Laguna as producer. Laguna, a New Yorker who'd studied classical piano since the age of five, was a typically inspired Peter Meaden choice. Who else would have matched a 35-year old rock 'n' roll poet from Birmingham with a producer whose credits included writing for the Ohio Express and the Lemon Pipers, playing keyboards for Tommy James and the Shondells ('Mony Mony'), composing the instrumental 'Groovin' With Mr. Bloe' and appearing either as a backing singer or musician on such bubblegum hits by the 1910 Fruitgum Company as 'Simon Says,' 'Goody Goody Gumdrops' and 'Indian Giver'?

'Tulane' was a high point both for the Steve Gibbons Band and for Peter but had the adverse effect of typecasting Gibbons as a cover artist and drawing attention away from his skills as a songwriter and lyricist. Follow-up singles didn't have the same commercial impact and he would never again return to the charts although he became a hard-working touring act, recorded well received albums and formed the successful side band he named The Dylan Project that played Dylan songs. Kenny Laguna went on to produce and manage Joan Jett's highly successful career.

By 1978 Peter's mood darkened yet further. He was brooding on apocalyptic scenarios and hearing voices in his head again. "People who use drugs to go up often come crashing down," says Keith Altham who'd first met Peter in 1964 and then reconnected with him as publicist for both The Who and Steve Gibbons. "There's a terrible counterbalance. I think he became almost manic depressive at stages." Gibbons remembers him running for a tube train on his way to Euston Station when he slipped and almost fell beneath its wheels. "It was strange," he says. "It felt almost as if he had wanted

Opposite: Peter at work in the offices of Trinifold Management, 114 Wardour Street

to die that way. That was the last time I saw him."

On July 6, 1978 he was admitted for a third time to hospital. The given reason was that he had become "increasingly withdrawn." His psychiatrist found no evidence of depression, psychotic illness or suicidal tendencies although Peter was reluctant to discuss the roots of his problems with staff. "He mainly kept himself to himself," reported the consultant, "but talked about a dilemma whether or not to leave home and get a flat in town." He wasn't prescribed any medication and when discharged on July 18 agreed to a follow up appointment in August.

While he was in hospital he found that Gina Strauss, his old girlfriend from the Hampstead days, was a fellow patient. Her life had followed a steady downward spiral since then. She'd married, divorced and become addicted to heroin. The young couple who'd once epitomised the delights of being young, adventurous and experimental were now two wrecks. Not long after she was on a train coming to London while her mind was confused by drugs and she opened the door and fell on to the tracks. The resulting injuries required the amputation of both her legs.

Completely out of the blue he reconnected with June Southworth, by then a feature writer on the *Daily Mail*. Her last contact with him had been in the mid-Sixties when she was with *Fabulous*. "He rang me and invited me out for a drink," she says. "We met and he told me he'd been in a psychiatric unit and that he'd had mental breakdowns brought on by drugs and drink.

Opposite:
Chris Chappel,
disguised as
Santa, with
Peter at a
Trinifold
Christmas
party

"There were certainly flashes of the old Peter. He wasn't a total wreck. He just looked as though he was fading. I don't think he had anything to sell me. He was just trying to make the best of the situation. I felt that he was saying goodbye to people. It was such a strange thing for him to ring me after not seeing me for over a decade."

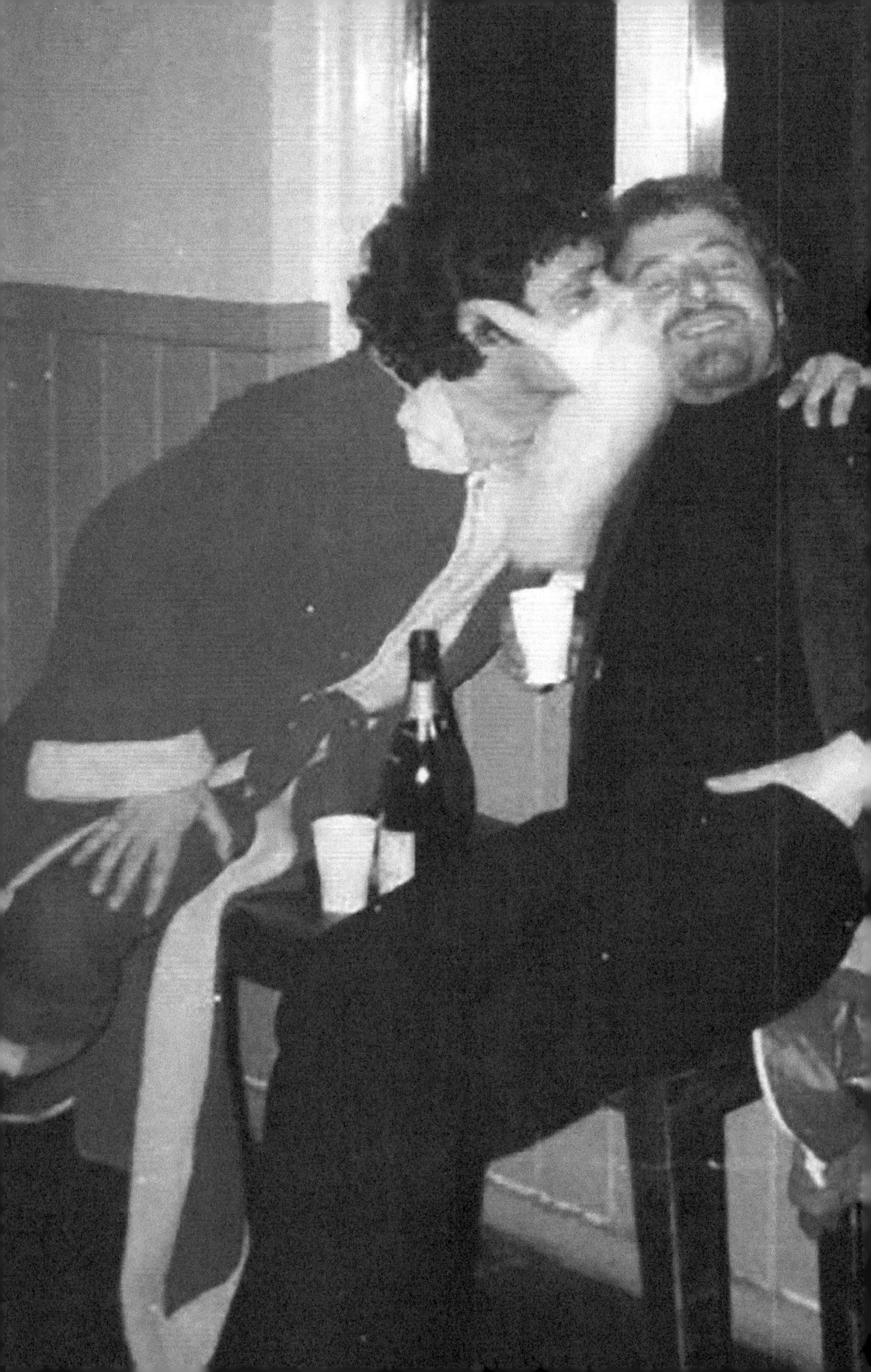

On Friday July 28 he left the house in Edmonton in the morning and returned at 3pm in the afternoon "in quite a state" according to his father. Already smelling of alcohol he consumed some port and a bottle of Pilsner lager in the living room. He then went out again and when he came back asked his father to buy him a bottle of whisky. He refused and so Peter went up to his room. Before doing so he handed his father his wristwatch saying; "This is for you." "He later called to me," remembered Stanley Meaden in his statement to the police, "and he told me that he had some work to do and that I was not to disturb him or to let his mother come near him."

Shortly after 8 am on the morning of July 30 Mr. Meaden could hear no movement coming from the room even though he could see from the gap beneath the door that the light was switched on. He tried to open the door, but something was wedged against it. He called Peter's name but there was no answer.

He called the police and at 8:15 PC Brian Maynard, out on patrol with WPC Hathaway, was given instructions to proceed to 7 Cuthbert Road. They arrived five minutes later and Mr. Meaden took them up to the first floor where Peter's bedroom was at the back of the house overlooking the garden.

PC Maynard pushed the door open and "found the apparently lifeless body of a man lying on the floor face down, his head against the door." The eyelids were swollen and there was dried fluid around the mouth. He was clutching an opened pack of cigarettes in one hand and a box of matches in the other. In a red holdall was an empty tablet bottle, on the bedside table a Seconal tablet. A finished bottle of vodka stood on the mantelpiece. There was no note even though there was a biro next to the bed. In death, as in life, he was impeccably dressed – a crisp white T-shirt, white socks and black pinstriped trousers. "The verdict was an open one, but he'd probably planned it," says Gerald Meaden. "He must have

Opposite: The author (left) with Steve Gibbons, Peter and Japanese photographer Herbie Yamaguchi. at the Rock Garden, London, November 5, 1976

known what he was doing.

"I suppose he'd had had enough of it all. At the time he was being asked to do a lot of work for the band and he couldn't cope with it all. There were a lot of dates to be booked and he just didn't want to do it. Just before he had come to stay with me in Brighton and he was behaving very strangely. My daughter was about three months old at the time and Peter was wandering around saying he was going to write about his life and then locking himself in his room for 24 hours at a time. We found him a bit creepy. My wife said, 'He's got to go.' So, he disappeared and went to stay with my parents."

Bill Curbishley told the police that Peter was obviously feeling under stress for the last two months of his life. After his last discharge "he didn't seem to want to work." Before travelling to America for business, Curbishley called him in for a serious conversation. "I had a long talk with him and pointed out that he would have to pull himself together. I told him that his work was suffering." It was while away that Curbishley heard that he had died. When his estate was finally settled in 1983 it was valued at only £3,791.

The inquest into the death opened on August 1, 1978, but was then adjourned until November 9 to get reports from a toxicologist and consultant psychiatrist. The toxicologist found that he had taken 12 Seconal tablets on top of the alcohol but concluded that an ordinary member of 'the public' would not necessarily know the actions of Seconal when mixed with alcohol. The psychiatrist, who knew Peter from Claybury, said that there was "no evidence of psychosis or hallucinations. He would have been responsible for his actions and of their effect." Coroner David Paul declared that death was by alcohol and barbiturate poisoning but that the verdict as to whether he'd intended to die or had just mistaken the dosage and its effect was "open."

Despite this, those close to him felt he knew far too much

about drugs to make a careless mistake. The shutting of the door, the warning to his parents not to come in his room and the ominous handing over of the watch to his father suggested a sense of purpose and a symbolic gesture of closure. "When I was living in Shepherd's Bush in the Seventies Peter would come over and we'd listen to Dion and The Belmonts," says John Emery. "He loved doing that. Then he'd say, 'I'm just about to board the Oblivion Express.' I asked him what this was. He said 'I take two sleeping tablets and a glass of vodka. Then, when I get home, I go to sleep.'"

When Jackie Curbishley cleared out his desk at Trinifold she found an exercise book that he'd completely filled with one sentence repeated over and over again. "Every page was covered with lines in the way they would be if you'd been given lines at school. It said, 'Jackie has a cat and she feeds it.' That was it. I've often pondered on that and tried to work out what it meant and why he would do that."

Less than six weeks later Keith Moon died as the result of an overdose of sedatives. As in Peter's case, the coroner couldn't conclusively declare that it was suicide and so the verdict was left open. Although The Who would carry on as a group this was the end of the iconic line-up. Twenty-four years later, on the verge of a US tour with The Who, John Entwistle would die in a Nevada hotel of a cocaine overdose.

Filming on *Quadrophenia* started a few weeks after Keith's death with Phil Daniels as the central character, Jimmy, and Sting as the Ace Face. When the film was released in late 1979 it would inspire new generations with the mod vision that owed so much to Peter's idea of "clean living under difficult circumstances" (a quote that was used on the album sleeve) and a band that could speak to, and on behalf of, a youth subculture.

The soundtrack album, fittingly, was dedicated to Peter Meaden.

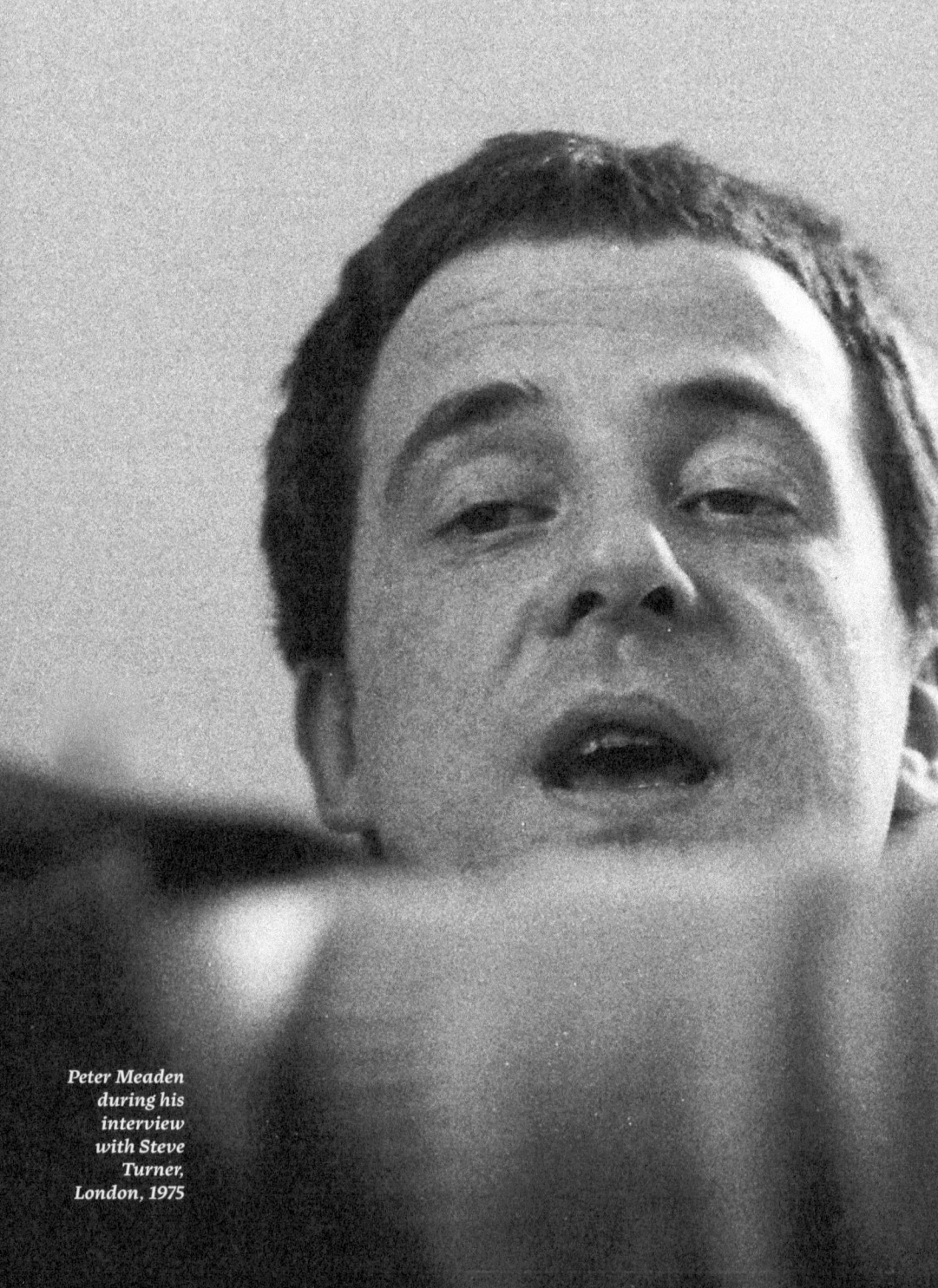

Peter Meaden during his interview with Steve Turner, London, 1975

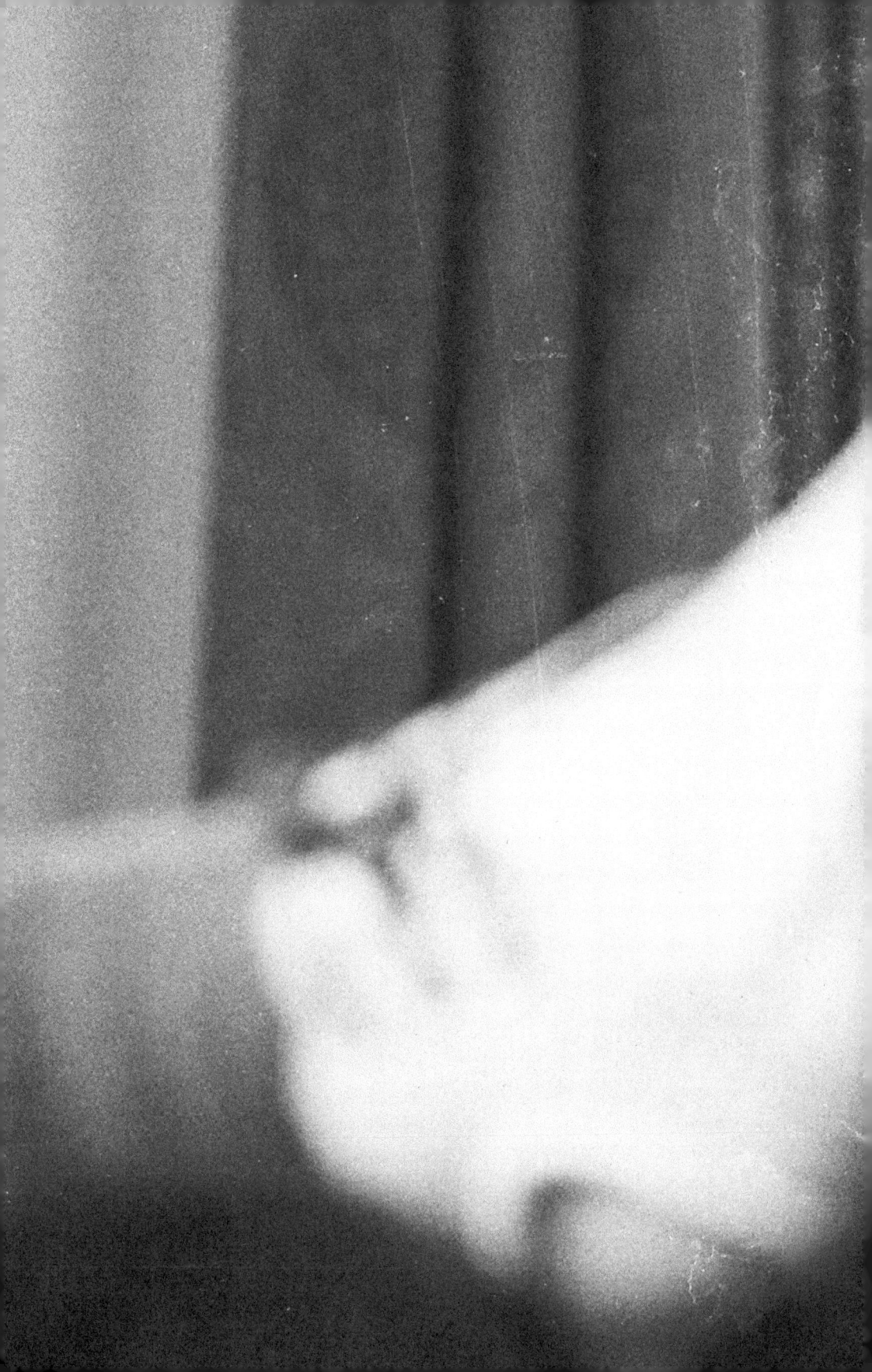

THE INTERVIEW

Existing is what it's all about because with society as we know it breaking down I think survival is of the utmost importance. It's all very well being immensely talented, having a good time and making great music, but if you can't sustain it... This sustaining bit is the most important of all and The Who are survivors. That's what I'm interested in, what I've always been interested in. I got out of business at the age of 14 by buying typewriters and selling them for three or four times what I paid for them, by sticking an advert in the papers and getting a shop which took them as part-exchange typewriters. So, business I was out of at the age of 14 only to find that morally it wasn't the right way to make a living and it couldn't be that easy.

I went into advertising which causes the survival of products so much as they market a product and it's no more interesting than any other product except that the box is better or the tube (if it's toothpaste) is better[1]. They cause the survival of a piece of product because they know the right marketing techniques. They know what reaches The Man. And this is what The Who is all about. I've got to say now, early on, that The Who's music is not alien to me. I mean, it has a big bass response and it picks up on me, but The Who's music is survival music.

Survival music is not necessarily the music that's exactly right on at any particular point in time, like a hit record. There was a long period of time when The Who didn't have any hit records at all. But their music is survival music by the pure power of sustaining. Sustaining power. That's what you have to say about The Who. This is what I built on in the very first place. I say 'I' because I don't think anyone has more effect on their career than me when I put together The High Numbers. I met them with a guy called Bob Druce[1] and

1 Druce ran a company called Commercial Entertainments Limited that booked acts into pubs and licensed clubs around London.

another fellow called Helmut Gorden[2]. Bob Druce was an agent who booked them, and he said he had a contract for The Who on his desk. I was introduced to The Who by my barber, via a mutual friend called Phil The Greek[3]. Phil The Greek was later to appear on *Ready Steady Go!*[4] with a sawn-off shotgun. He was one of the great legends of folklore and pop history.

What was his role?

He was the fellow who said, "Listen Peter..." We used to go to The Scene club[5] together. He was a mod. This was in '63, '64. Oh, this is my mod jacket.

How long have you had it?

Oh no. Sorry. This is the wrong one. It's a new one. I've got some mod socks.

Does that mean you think the mod thing is still alive?

I wonder actually where all the old mods went. They're probably all in garages, second-hand car outfits, scrapyards. Things like that. There's such a thing as 'mod suss.' You know– sussing out a situation. That's what mods are all about. They suss a situation out immediately – its potential and how to control it, rather than sitting down and letting the potential control them. The mods always controlled the situation. So, I would think they'd get into the car game. That's where the most money is made very quickly.

Are you still in touch with any of your old mates?

Yeh. One's a coke dealer, one's in prison, and another one is the guy who appeared on television with a shotgun with The Who on *Ready Steady Go!*[6] He was the greatest mod leader of them all – Phil The Greek. Pete Townshend and I talk about him often. Another

Opposite: Peter said that Philip Andronicos, known as Phil the Greek, was the "flashiest mod I knew." He is pictured in 1966 by which time he was working for the Vidal Sassoon Academy in London

2 Helmut Gorden (1915-1990) was a Jewish immigrant from Eastern Europe who ran a brass foundry in Shepherd's Bush, West London, and had aspirations to break into show business management in emulation of Beatles' manager Brian Epstein.

3 'Phil The Greek' was Philip Andronicos (1945-   ). He denies the *Ready Steady Go!* story but admits an incident in Trowbridge, Wiltshire, when he was working for The Pretty Things. He had a gun in his car boot as he used to go skeet shooting. Surrounded by threatening rockers outside Trowbridge Town Hall he pulled it out to scare the mob away and was promptly arrested.

4 *Ready Steady Go!* (1963-1966) was created by the independent television production company Associated Rediffusion. It was screened live on Friday evenings on ITV between 6:00 pm and 7:00 pm..

5 The Scene club was a basement club run by Ronan O'Rahilly and Lionel Blake at Ham Yard, 41 Great Windmill Street, in London's Soho.

6 See footnote 3 re. the shotgun.

of my mod friends is Mickey Tenner[7] who's a dealer in all sorts of things. He goes into companies that make Rank Xerox go bust for £20,000. He makes £3,000 out of a bankrupt company. He had a company called Exciting Lighting. That's what 'mod suss' is all about. It's checking out a situation, enjoying it for what it's worth and then splitting. If you were a mod bull-fighter you'd have twenty – or seven or eight or nine – of your mod friends and when the bull came out you'd have a dirty great ten foot pole with a great bolt on it. As the bull came out you'd whack him on the mouth with it and he'd go 'donk'! You'd drop him because you wouldn't want mod friends to get their nice smart clothes all spoilt. Then you'd glance around and cut the bollocks off, and the ears off or whatever, and give them to your mates. You'd never give them to a bird. That's what the mods were all about. It really is that. They'd conk that bull before he even got near their mates – right in the doorway as he came out into the ring. It's playing safe.

Do you think they've fared well?

The spade girls are the mod chicks of today – those little spade chicks you see running around in stacked heels and wedges wearing Ossie Clarke[8] clothes. The blacks were always there in '64 but there weren't so many of them. They were late night kids like us. You'd go out on a three-day bender. You'd hit out on a Friday night, high on speed, go down to *Ready Steady Go!*[9], then on to The Scene club and dance all night 'til Saturday morning. On Saturday you'd go shopping to buy a pullover or a scarf or something – a pair of socks 'cos your feet hurt dancing all night in desert boots[10] – and then through to Saturday night again

Opposite: Peter with Jimmy James (top right) and six Vagabonds. The band represented Peter's attempt to recapture the mod market after losing control of The Who

7 Michael Tenner (1947 -   ) was a great dancer and a regular at The Scene club where he was known as Mickey the Monkey because of his dancing style, especially when moving to 'Monkey Time' by Major Lane.
8 Raymond 'Ossie' Clarke (1942-1996) began designing for Alice Pollock's boutique Quorum in 1966. He became known for designs that took their inspiration from vintage fashion.
9 At the time *Ready Steady Go!* was filmed live from Studio 9 at Television House on the corner of London's Aldwych and Kingsway. The building had previously been Adastral House, home to the Air Ministry during World War 2. It later became St Catherine's House where the General Register Office was based. It has now been renamed Centrium and houses many different companies.
10 Desert boots were crepe-soled shoes with two lace holes and a high ankle surround. They were developed by Clarks in 1950 and were based on shoes that British soldiers were having made in the bazaars of Cairo during World War II. The inventor, Nathan Clark, has said: "I got the idea from crepe soled rough suede boots worn by officers in the Eighth Army."

140

at The Scene club through to Sunday morning. That's when the comedown would come down because you can't sustain it much more than three days - two nights, three days. Then you start heading home to Mama's place. You live at home because you can't afford to live anywhere else other than Mama's place. You crash round about Sunday morning if you get a lift home to North London, where I was[11]. And that was the life. It was the most amazing sort of life you could imagine! It was so amazing to be a mod. It was the finest. You had Drinamyl[12]. They make amphetamine differently these days which means that it lasts about four or five hours and you can sleep on it. The amphetamine I'm talking about was real rough stuff. The blisters would come up on your tongue and on your lips, but you could knock on for three days without sleeping and you wouldn't feel anything. Comedowns. All comedowns were emotional breakthroughs coming through. This is what Townshend talks about in his songs. I talk about it in my way. Emotional breakthroughs are realising and experiencing emotional setbacks, which cause you to feel ill, sad and lonely. This is what the mod thing was. It was the unity of modism which interested me so much. This is why I personally got together something like 240,000-250,000 mods in '64 and '67 who used to knock around the south coast and up and down the country. I had Jimmy James and The Vagabonds[13], which was a purist mod band. The Who became the focus of mods. There was something like 250,000 revolutionary kids, which is like the Vietcong[14] out there when Hanoi didn't fall, and Saigon did.

What do you mean you got them together?

I got them together in that I loved the life so much that I got

Opposite: Mickey Tenner (left) outside the Scene Club in 1964. He became a regular dancer at Ready Steady Go! *and later worked for* Radio Caroline

11 Meaden lived with his parents in a terraced house in Cuthbert Road in Edmonton.
12 Known as Purple Hearts, Frenchies, doobs and various other names these tablets included amphetamine and barbiturate. They came onto the market in 1950 and were manufactured by Smith, Kline & French.
13 Jimmy James (1940 -   ) formed his group in Jamaica and came to Britain in May 1964. Jimmy James and The Vagabonds became a resident group at the Marquee in Soho's Wardour Street in 1965.
14 The Viet Cong was the National Front for the Liberation of South Vietnam. It fought a guerrilla war against American troops.

The Who together. I got The Who and I dressed them up in mod clothes. I gave them all the jingoism and paraphernalia of modism – boxing boots and fashionable things. Right on the button. Timing just right. 'Cos timing is where it's at.

You were already a mod by then?

Yeh. I was a mod. It was my life.

What were the mods?

There was a little club called The Scene club in Ham Yard off Great Windmill Street and there on several nights a week the greatest records you can imagine were being played. There were records like 'Ain't Love Good, Ain't Love Proud' by Tony Clarke[15] and Major Lance's[16] stuff and early Curtis Mayfield and The Impressions[17] stuff, you know, which was eminently danceable to by people who were not emotionally involved with other people. There was a lack of women in those things. I mean we all dig women, but if you're in the West End you know that you'll pay for your women and, well, you don't get them because the girls that come up are mysteries, right? You get the girls who come up and dance around, little girls who just dance around in the pubs, just having a little groove. Well everyone's having a groove and you can have a groove without an emotional tangle-up – tango-up – 'cos that's what you do. You tango, you dance – you know? So, you 'dance to keep from crying' which was one of the main records of that period. That was Smokey Robinson and The Miracles, right, and that was a big record in America, not so big in England[18]. It wasn't a big hit here at all. But it was coming up at the same time as The Beatles were coming up. Now The Beatles were coming up in America. Now the mods, you must realise, were anti-heroes, they were

Opposite: Peter discovered The Scene in 1963. "There on several nights a week the greatest records you can imagine were being played."

15 Tony Clarke (1944-1971) wrote hits for Etta James before having his own hit 'The Entertainer' in 1965. He was killed by his estranged wife in an act of self defence.

16 Major Lance (1941-1994) was born in Mississippi but raised in Chicago. He went to the same high school as musicians Curtis Mayfield and Jerry Butler. He had a US hit in 1963 with 'The Monkey Time'.

17 Actually known as The Impressions but featuring Curtis Mayfield.

18 'I Gotta Dance to Keep From Crying' by The Miracles was released on October 31 1963 by Motown Records. It was written by Holland-Dozier-Holland. In the USA it reached # 35 in the Billboard charts and #17 in the R&B charts.

anti the hero, because their heroes were much more personal. They were touchable, reachable, and The Beatles were going out very big. I recently saw a reprint of a *Cashbox*[19] front page and it had the first record, 'Love Me Do,' by The Beatles, and on the next line, directly across from it, was 'I Gotta Dance to Keep from Crying' by Smokey and The Miracles. And that was one of the greatest records. That was where they would pull out all sorts of stops in the recording studios, in the studio where they were working[20]. They would pull out everything but the bass line. Just the bass line would be going on and then they'd put it back up again, pushing up all the slides on the deck, so it was like a semi-psychedelic record[21]. Played very loud over those big speakers which were like fairground speakers, in a small room with concrete walls which was The Scene club, it would come bouncing back, hitting off the floor. There was no wood on the floor. It would then hit off the ceiling, so you were getting saturated by sound, and they'd pull down all the stops. You were getting a psychedelic record –and this was in '64! That's why Motown[22] is a groovy company. They know that if you hit a person on his bass responses – hit in on his feet and up his legs – you're getting a physical reaction. Then you come in with the guitar and you're hitting inward with the bass drum, the lead guitar hits in the head and the piano hits in the head alone. So, you're picking up on a body all the way through. This is what mods are about. They're physical. They're physical people. They're not just heads. A 'Head'[23] is a person who's had his physical senses sucked up into his head and has forgotten about his body. He drapes his body in the most colourful clothes be can because he's not proud of his body, or he's ashamed of his

19 *Cashbox* was an American trade paper for the music industry.
20 The record was produced at the Motown studio in Detroit by Brian Holland and Lamont Dozier.
21 Meaden is referring to the central section of the track where the instruments are faded down and then swiftly brought back up again. It was recorded to sound as if a party was in process.
22 Motown was started in Detroit by Berry Gordy in 1959. The soulish vocals, great dance rhythms and powerful bass lines were loved by the mods. In the UK its releases first appeared on the London, Fontana, Oriole American and Stateside labels before EMI created the Tamla Motown label in 1965.
23 A 'head' was an abbreviation for either a pot-head or an acid-head, someone whose life and thinking was dominated by the mental effects of a particular drug.

body or he doesn't even think about his body. He thinks only in his head. That's what a freak is, you know. I'm talking about people who are freaks. When I first took acid, Townshend made me. I laid Drinamyl on Townshend[24]. I was the first person to lay Purple Hearts on him. He laid acid on me in '67. I was one of the first people to get the real good L. A. stuff, the L. A. Blues. It was Owsley[25] acid with speed in it so you could get through the guilt complex straight away and get into the real acid right on, you know? It was Owsley acid and that was great. But Drinamyl is a drug for mods because it's a functional drug. It's a drug you can work on, you can steal from shops on it, do all the things you need to do. You can dance on it. You lose all lack of confidence. You lose guilt. It opens up the capillary vessels in the body so you became aware of your system[26]. You become aware of your body and therefore with the aid of this drug you have your own society. You have nirvana in a single little purple pill. Plus, you've got good togs – nice clothes – which is what it's all about. You have the confidence, plus you have the sustaining power of two nights up, three days up. I think it's a groove. I think it's fabulous, man!

When did you first notice this happening?

When my doctor gave me Drinamyl I was a freelance commercial artist. My partner was Andrew Oldham[27] and we worked together for a while in a company called Image and we were doing a brochure for Sportique – this was John Michael Ingram[28]. We got all this stuff through and we had a thing called *Sportique*

---

24 Meaden later corrects this statement. After our first conversation he phoned Pete Townshend and got Townshend's side of the story.

25 Owsley acid was LSD manufactured by the enigmatic Owsley Stanley (b. 1935) who began production in the San Francisco area in May 1965 with 300,000 capsules. It was recognised as being the purest and most powerful form of LSD available at the time.

26 It actually raises blood pressure, constricts blood vessels and dilates the small bronchial sacs.

27 Andrew Loog Oldham (1944 -) was to make his name by managing The Rolling Stones and constructing their bad boy image. He mentions Meaden frequently in his autobiography Stoned.

28 John Michael Ingram (1931-2014) was a designer who established Sportique at 170 Kings Road, Chelsea, in 1957. He then opened a branch at 63 Old Compton Street in Soho. He had started in women's fashion and wanted colour and style in the clothes worn by British men. He introduced shoes without laces, took the bagginess out of trousers and pioneered 'matching gear'. He later opened stores called Guy and John Michael in other London locations.

PAN GIANT

On the Road

Jack Kerouac

Explosive epic of the Beat Generation

Wild and unrestrained
EVENING STANDARD

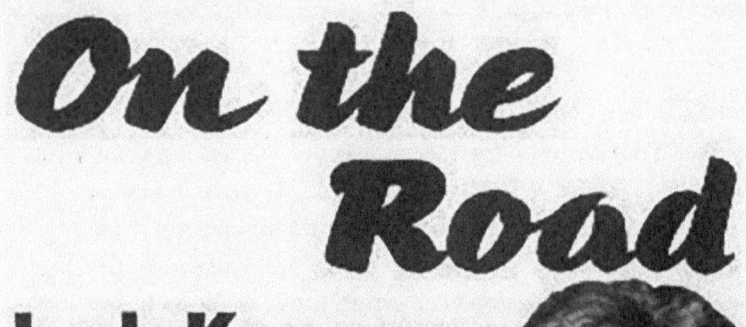

3'6

Takes a Holiday, a brochure[29]. So, I did the design. I was doing the drawings and just getting an anxiety block. I couldn't put my view of it on paper without getting a headache, without thinking "I could do with a drink, I could do with this..." I was in my early twenties and I went around to my doctor and said, "Look. I've got to do this work. I've got a whole lot of things I have to do, and I just can't do it. I'm getting physical headaches in the act of creation. I just can't put pen to paper without these boredom thrusts filling me up." I went through the anxiety bit and so my doctor said, "Well, I'll prescribe these then" and she gave me the original Drinamyl, the original Purple Hearts. She gave me twenty or thirty on the National Health for two bob and I went back to my parents' house where I was working from, got out the pills and took one. It was just like medicine. I thought it would probably do something physically way down in my system and I'd never notice it. Then suddenly BANG!! I'm free! I was unburdened of the chains of resistance. I was able to write and draw and do all the things I wanted to do without the restraints of normal civilisation bothering me, which is like feeling that it's late and having to go to bed. It was all just as simple as that. I sat up all though the night and finished the brochure in that one night.

Were pills very popular then?

No. Well this is how I discovered pills. I found the pills. This was in 1962.

Mods didn't exist?

No, they weren't in existence – but Jack Kerouac[30] was. So, anyway, I took the Drinamyl. I finished the brochure in a night and I was up for three nights trying to wear my energy off. They give amphetamines to kids these days to boost their intelligence. They say that something happens as you get

29 This was for a forthcoming spring collection and is remembered by Andrew Loog Oldham in *Stoned.*
30 *On the Road* was first published in Britain in 1958. Kerouac was known to enjoy writing while high on amphetamine. He would extract the amphetamine soaked wadding from the plastic Benzedrine Inhaler and drop it into a cup of coffee. He felt that this enabled him to express himself more spontaneously as it temporarily rid him of his self-censoring mechanisms.

Opposite Meadon was inspired by Kerouc's On the Road to live life in the fast lane. Kerouac was a lover of black music, 'mad' people, and Benzedrine

older. Now this isn't true. They've changed amphetamines from the rough amphetamine you used to get. You can get street amphetamine which is really rough. It doesn't last very long but has the same sustaining power as the early stuff. They call them Frenchies because they're made by Smith, Kline and French[31] and this is the basis of the mod thing. It's so unique. There was old Jack Kerouac with his Benzedrine inhalers. When I was fourteen I was trying to distill caffeine and make Benzedrine. After reading Jack Kerouac I went down and bought Benzedrine inhalers and just tried to swallow them with the aromatics.

Hadn't the inhalers been modified by then?

Yes. They changed them. There was no Benzedrine in them, but the aromatics went up my nostrils and I was tearing my hair out. I used to distill caffeine and buy Pro Plus[32] and stuff like that. You've got to realise that it's a drug society. The thing that amphetamine does, as you're probably aware, is to block the nerve ends after about a year.

So, you stop being responsive?

No. It's not that. There's a tolerance level on amphetamine. You can't take more than four. After that it starts getting a bit muzzy. I have a doctor in town that I go to and he prescribes me Dexedrine. You can't get Drinamyl anymore, or you can't get it very easily. I have to grumble if I want some off him. I'm not a speed freak but I appreciate the power of nirvana in a single tablet. Unlike acid or heroin or pot, Drynamil has just enough barbiturate to take the edge and the nervousness off the amphetamine buzz. It gives you a good high, and then you're free. You're a 'Fremen' just like in Dune[33]. That's interesting. It makes society viable. Life doesn't have to be a dull, mundane existence.

Would you prescribe pills for everyone if you could?

31 Smith, Kline and French was an American pharmaceutical company with origins in early 19th century Philadelphia. It developed the Benzedrine Inhaler in the Twenties as a bronchial dilator. It is now a part of GlaxoSmithKline.
32 Pro Plus is a brand of 'pep pill' available without a prescription. Its main stimulant is caffeine.
33 *Dune* was a 1965 novel by Frank Herbert (1920-1986)

I'd put 15 tons on the street right away. No, not right away! I'd have to do it tactically. It's all down to tactics.

It sounds like an Aldous Huxley novel.[34]

It's not Aldous Huxley. It's not a speed freak novel either because all speed freaks get into Hitler[35]. I'm talking genuinely. Look, society as we know it is going to break down in two years. It has to. It cannot stand the pace. It can't stand the strain of money when there is no money. No one wants to borrow money. No one wants to pay interest on any money. No one wants to buy any houses. Transactions aren't going on. Beef is £2 per lb or whatever it costs these days. A pound per lb at least. It's getting horrific. I'm now in a place where I can test out stress things because I discovered some time ago that if you intentionally put stress into situations you get a reciprocal effect back. It's almost a mathematical thing. I'm not a mathematician but if you inject stress into a situation into an ordinary relationship, stress on a nice high octave level, and you hit it down low but not too much, you find that especially with women it comes back even more. If I try being nice with women, I find it doesn't work. I've been married for nine years and I've just got the divorce going through.[36] That was just a nice guy trip. I was just being nice to a chick and nothing happened out of it. Women will destroy the volition of a man. That's the important word. Volition is the impulse to move forward. A woman has no impulse like volition. She'll not help a man move forward. Volition is the will to move forward and women don't have volition. Now this is what speed gives you and this is what the mods are all about. This is going back to the mods and going back to The Who. Speed gives you the volition inasmuch as it gives the image

34 In *Brave New World* Aldous Huxley (1894-1963) wrote of a future society where inner peace was provided to citizens through a drug called Soma. Huxley described the fictitious drug as having, "All the advantages of Christianity and alcohol; none of their defects."

35 Re-reading the interview I was struck by how often he referred to the need for purity and precision. In his latter years he was very keen on the book *Spear of Destiny* (1973) by Trevor Ravenscroft (1921-1989) which proposed that magical powers inhabited the spear that had pierced the side of Christ and that Hitler tried to track the weapon down as part of his search for world domination.

36 Meaden married Wendy Young (1945 -   ) in 1967 and they had a son, Sacha Benedict Meaden, who was born in 1968. Sacha is now a successful painter living in London.

that there's a life worth living outside of the ordinary mundane existence. There is an escape route with the pill and the pill is Drinamyl. It has to be this precise because there are all sorts of different amphetamines. There's Methedrine[37], real rough amphetamine sulphate that you can snort up your nose. There's Dexedrine, which is dexamphetamine. They are all different, tactically slightly different sorts of things. You have to have the groove to go on, to keep the weekend going. It's like the kick-start on a motorcycle. You have to kick it down to have that grip, like the abrasive surface on a matchbox. You just move forward, you keep moving forward, and that's what the mod thing is. It's always moving forward. You ask old Townshend this. He'll tell you. I see The Who as that famous painting[38] by that French painter about 1918 of the machine gun which is always full-speed ahead, headlong speed, plus a few other words which indicate thrust, vibration, stuff like that. It's of three or four men locked around a machine gun on a stand. It's in the First World War, in the trenches with the barbed wire around it, with a sort of modernistic approach. That's what The Who is all about. That's what mods are all about. It's the headlong thrust into the unknown, a quest into the unknown. (Addresses the tape recorder) Townshend – show us your toe laces. That's all I want to see. Turn this thing off. (At this point it seemed that he was considering whether he had been too open and enthusiastic about his drug intake during the interview. He returned with a warning). My own personal feeling is that the debt you have to pay for drugs is too much to compensate for taking the drugs in the first place. I would say, don't take any drugs whatsoever. A few smokes, a few beers, take speed a little bit now and again, but be careful with everything else. That's all.

Did you see yourself as the King Mod?

37 Methylamphetamine

38 He must have been thinking of La Mitrailleuse (1915) which, despite its French title, was by the British painter C. R. W. Nevinson (1889-1946). The poet and art critic Apollinaire said that it "translates the mechanical aspect of modern warfare where man and machine combine to form a single force of nature." It hangs at the Tate Gallery in London.

Opposite "I see The Who as that famous painting of the machine gun that is always full-speed ahead, headlong speed, plus a few other words…" La Mitrailleuse by Christopher Nevinson (1915)

No. I was the fellow who saw the potential in mod-ism, which is the greatest form of lifestyle you can imagine. It's so totally free. It's so totally anti family London in so much as there were lonely ordinary people having a groovy time, having a great time, not having to be lonely, not having to worry about relationships, and being able to get into the most fantastic, interesting, beautiful situations, just out of music. You could dance by yourself. You could groove around. Imagine this – on a Friday night I would go down to *Ready Steady Go!*, I would groove around there. One weekend I had three people on *Ready Steady Go!* – The Crystals, Chuck Berry and The Rolling Stones[39]. I was doing publicity for all three acts. They used to say 'The weekend begins here' (sic)[40] and the weekend would begin there. I'd take my speed, I'd go down there, and go up to the Green Room, then watch the people I was working for have a great time on television. There'd be all the faces and people I knew there. A 'face' is just someone you recognise. That's all a face means – someone you recognise. You might even know his name, but he's known as a Face.

Is that why you titled the first single (for The Who as The High Numbers) 'I Am the Face'?

Yeh. 'I Am the Face' is one of those people who is familiar. It's a familiar thing. A face can be a familiar face to other people. *Ready Steady Go!* was interesting inasmuch as it got the vibe right out with a good edge on it. There were always so many kids outside trying to get in that you had to thrust your way though with a lot of hard chat into the main foyer of ATV House down there in the Strand. You'd go to the Green Room first and have a few sherbets[41] to round the edge off the Drinamyl and then down into *Ready Steady Go!* where there'd be Mickey Tenner, Phil the Greek and a few other faces dancing around with some of the

39 All three acts were never on *Ready Steady Go!* together but the Stones and The Crystals appeared on the same show on February 14, 1964, The Stones performed 'Not Fade Away', 'I Wanna Be Your Man' and 'You Better Move On.'
40 'The weekend starts here', not 'begins here', was the slogan of *Ready Steady Go!*
41 Beers.

girls[42]. There'd be Sandy Sarjeant[43], who is Mickey Tenner's wife now (sic), and Cathy McGowan[44]. There'd be the Stones around, or The Who, or maybe Paul Jones and Manfred Mann[45], and that would be a great fillip for the weekend to start off on. That would be enough to make a nice edge. That would be exciting enough to make a nice edge like the kick-start on a motorbike. You push it down. You don't pump it or anything like that. You pump it just to fill it up to see that you get enough gas into the cylinder, then you kick it WHOMP! And she starts firing, and you move off into the weekend.

What happened on Saturdays?

On Saturday? After Friday night, after *Ready Steady Go!* and after seeing the rock and roll things, the stars and that, it was always the same. It didn't matter. Have a few drinks, then you split, take a taxi into town, the West End, groove around for a bit, go to a pub in Great Windmill Street, have a few drinks. I used to drink cider. That would affect with the barbiturate to make it mellowing. Now, you must remember that I was called a 'pilled up mod' by a man called Tony Hall[46] who didn't realise the potential that this single little drug has on a revolutionary society. Anyway, that's another thing. We'd go down to The Scene club and I would listen to records. There'd be Guy Stevens[47] there. He wouldn't be playing on a Friday night, but

42 The dancers were carefully selected from young London clubs and so the programme became a showcase for hairstyles, clothing, dances and music that was cool in the city. The studio's green room was a fashionable hang-out for music industry movers and shakers.

43 Althea 'Sandy' Sarjeant (1947 -   ) was a resident dancer on *Ready Steady Go!* and later on Germany's *Beat Club*. In London she shared a flat with P. P. Arnold. She made a promotion-only single for German Polydor in 1967 ('Can't Stop the Want') and married Small Faces' keyboard player Ian McLagan in 1968. They had one child before divorcing in 1972. She was never married to Mickey Tenner.

44 Cathy McGowan (1943 -   ) was the show's main presenter. She responded to an advert asking for a 'typical teenager' to act as an advisor on a new music programme. At the time she was working in the fashion department of the weekly magazine *Woman's Own*. She has lived with the British singer Michael Ball since 1992.

45 Manfred Mann was the keyboard player in the group that bore his name. The group's vocalist was Paul Jones. Their single '5-4-3-2-1' was used at the theme music for *Ready Steady Go!* in its early days.

46 Tony Hall worked in the promotion department of Decca Records. Meaden returns to this episode later in the interview and suggests that it was a catalyst in his determination to succeed with The Who. In Andrew Loog Oldham's autobiography *Stoned*, Hall is quoted as saying "I always thought Peter Meaden was a genius."

47 Guy Stevens (1943-1981) was the resident DJ at The Scene cluband his rare US R&B imports, set the tone for the music that was appreciated by the mods. Bands like The Who, The Rolling Stones and The Small Faces used his collection as source material for their cover versions. Stevens was responsible for naming the bands Procol Harum and Mott the Hoople and producing the classic Clash album *London Calling* in 1979.

he'd probably be sitting there. There'd be H, and there'd be a girl whose name I've forgotten who was a GI chick[48]. She liked the black GIs and would have all the soul records, you know, like Tony Clarke's 'Aint Love Good, Ain't Love Proud'[49] and all those really heavy danceable Seventies – not Fifties – dance rhythms. The Seventies dance rhythms were entirely different. They were very early Motownish, like Smokey Robinson and The Miracles and The Impressions. That lift/move thing. Then you're totally alone in The Scene club, Friday night, which was great because Friday night was much better than Saturday night. On Friday night you knew you had Saturday night to follow and what follows after Saturday night is Sunday night and you know Sunday night is a drag because you know you've got work on a Monday morning. So, on Friday night you have the anticipation of the whole weekend ahead of you, of excitement and thrills.

Didn't you sleep at all?

No, you didn't sleep at all. You stayed up all night.

What about Saturday morning?

Well, Saturday morning is a bit grotty because you sort of groove around the West End, do down to Cecil Gee's [on Shaftesbury Avenue][50] to see if you can get a belt or something. You groove around a bit, and hang out, and you talk a bit and you wander around a have a sandwich or something. You maybe go down the pub around lunchtime – well, around eleven o clock as a matter of fact. You have a drink, take a couple more tabs, purple hearts, blues, Frenchies, doobies, whatever you want to call them. Then you groove on through to Saturday afternoon when you sit around in some park, if there's nothing else to do, and

48 Meaden later recalls the girl was named Sandra. The Flamingo in Wardour Street was a favourite hangout for black American servicemen who were a prized source of cool records. They introduced a lot of rare R&B music to London musicians and music fans.
49 'Ain't Love Good, Ain't Love Proud' was released on the Chess label in 1964.
50 Cecil Gee established a men's clothing store on Charing Cross Road in 1929. He introduced the American look to men's leisurewear in the Forties and then, after a trip to Rome in 1956, the Italian look for men's casual suits. Influenced by designers such as Canali and Brioni he experimented with lightweight, more versatile fabrics that were ideal for dancing in. At the time, against a background of austerity, these were considered controversial and not 'manly' enough. Men weren't supposed to care so much about design detail and quality of material.

then fool around until Saturday might. Then, when the pubs were open, you'd head into the West End territory, which is just off Piccadilly Circus, and it was so private. When you're in your own private world it's very private indeed. There is no such thing as tourists. You just see gangs of fellow friends, faces, storming up and down Great Windmill Street and around the West End. A mod can recognise another mod just like that.

Did you see the potential of making The Who a focal point for all this?
Yeh. They were the focal point because I was thinking about revolution. I was thinking that society was great when you had speed, a couple of pints of cider and you're completely enveloped in music, in sounds. If you could add the visual impact of a really tough group, which is what I wanted, then you had The Who, you had The High Numbers. They were known as The High Numbers and that was the focal point of mod-ism.

Tell me about when you first met The Who.
A friend of mine called Phil the Greek who was the flashiest mod that I knew. He was the mod leader in so much that he wore a dark blue suit, a mohair suit, and he used to come down with me to The Scene club and we used to go to the same barber called Jack[51] who was in Marble Arch, just near Seymour Place, just near the Pye building[52].

Did he give good mod cuts?
No. He was just a barber who would do what you wanted him to do which is how barbers should be, not like a guy at Crimpers[53] or somewhere telling you how he thinks your hair should be. Now if you go to those Jewish barbers, they do your hair just right, just as you ask them. Now that's an important thing because I used to go along there to have my hair cut and Phil said to me that Jack had a group or that he knew of a group that was interesting and I'd been thinking of finding a group.

51 Lionel 'Jack' Marks whose Barber's Shop was at 97 Edgware Road, London.
52 Pye Records was a British label founded in the Fifties. Its HQ was at ATV House, Great Cumberland Place, close to Marble Arch.
53 Crimpers was a 'unisex' hair salon, one of the first, opened on Baker Street by Lawrence Falk, formerly of Vidal Sassoon.

Did the group get their hair cut there?

No. They didn't get their hair cut there. Phil the Greek and me went along to that barber to have our hair cut and for some months before I had been thinking very seriously about how I could get the focus, for my feelings, and the feelings of other people around me who were a hard-core group of mods who used to go to The Scene club in Ham Yard. The club was owned by Ronan O'Rahilly of Radio Caroline[54] fame at the time but it was run by a fellow called Lionel Blake[55]. Now that was a real hardcore fashion situation or system, call it what you will, as a position of glory. I used to go down there – it was very private – to dance by myself to the music which was sort of new wave R & B. Anyway, getting back to The Who; I loved the mods so much. I used to wear Ivy League suits[56] and American jackets and button-down collars and bottom-end shoes like desert boots or heavy suede shoes that later turned into Hush Puppies[57]. They were like dancing boots, like the Paras wear these days – combat boots – but they were made out of suede and were comfortable. They were light and functional. I was taking pills in so much as I had been introduced to pills by my doctor for the anxiety thing. I took some Drinamyl and it kept me up for three days and I zoomed around on that. I had such a great time, a fabulous time. Anyway, there was a whole *kultur*, which is German for culture but can't be accurately translated in less than fourteen sentences. Anyway, so there was my culture and I had my haircut there and the barber said to me that he had a group and I was thinking "How am I going to spread the word about this good

Opposite: Lionel Blake was at various times an accountant, war photographer, film extra and manager of The Scene club. He hired the DJs Sandra Blackstone and Guy Stevens and used Peter Meaden's knowledge of mod culture. Photo taken by the author in 2014. Blake died in 2018

54 Radio Caroline was a pirate radio ship that was positioned in international waters off the coast of Felixtowe, Suffolk, and began broadcasting to Britain on Easter Sunday 1964. Ronan O' Rahilly (1940-2020) was an Irish-born entrepreneur.
55 Lionel Robert Blake (1937 - 2018) was the co-manager. He was an extra in the film *Operation Crossbow* (1965) starring Sophia Loren.
56 Ivy League fashion grew up in America in the late Fifties. It was associated with university campuses and consisted of natural fabrics, button down collar shirts, loafers, trousers without pleats and natural shouldered single-breasted jackets.
57 Hush Puppies were a product of an American company named Wolverine who discovered a unique method of pigskin tanning in 1958 while working on footwear for the military. They were brushed-suede shoes with lightweight crepe souls and were given their name by the company's first sales manager James Gaylord Muir.

life that I am living?" I would go out with ten bob[58], my doctor's pills in my pocket which was two bob on the National Health. She would give me 30 a month – Drinamyl, Purple Hearts, the triangular ones with the line down the middle. The groove in the middle! And I would stay out for as long as I wanted to with all this energy. So anyway, I was living this lovely life of Riley where I was dancing to music that I liked, where you didn't have to get hung up on birds. Early mods never did. Well, they used to go out with birds down at the Tottenham Royal[59] but I used to go down to The Scene and it was very private, very dark. I used to go down there with Brian Jones[60]. I took Chuck Berry down there and a few people like that. I took Chuck to my parents' house once, after a show at the Edmonton Regal[61]. The Animals used to play at The Scene club and the Stones appeared. That was exactly purism mod which was a society unto itself. As I say, modism, mod living, is an aphorism for clean living under difficult circumstances, or different circumstances. You have your own values, your own set of time scales, your own units of existence, which are 'to have a good time, because it's alright' as the old Curtis Mayfield and The Impressions song goes. There are so many lines like, 'When you wake up early in the morning/ Feeling sad like so many of us do/ Hum a little soul/Make life your goal/ and surely something's gonna come to you/ And say it's alright/ Have a good time/ 'Cos it's all right.'[62] Well, that's what the mod thing was all about. It was just having a good time with your own drug which would keep you up. Now this is all a backlog to get us back to The Who. I'd been thinking it out. I'd been knocking around with The Rolling Stones. Andrew Oldham – Andrew Loog Oldham, the manager of The Rolling Stones – was my business partner in a company called Image. I

58 A 'bob' was slang for a shilling (5p) in pre-decimal currency.
59 The Tottenham Royal stood at 415-419 High Road, Tottenham, London N17. Built in the early twentieth century it had been a skating rink, a cinema and a jazz spot before being taken over by Mecca Dance Ltd who renamed it the Tottenham Royal. It became a well known dance venue. It was torn down in 2004.
60 Brian Jones (1942-1969) was a founder member of The Rolling Stones and a blues aficionado.
61 January 31, 1965.
62 'It's All Right' by The Impressions was released in 1963 on ABC Paramount.

thought the name up and we called it Image Limited. We were doing things and I went away to Spain for seven months, came back from Spain, met the Stones on my first morning back when they were recording 'Come On' and 'Money' at Decca, West Hampstead. It became their first hit.[63] I saw Andrew in the studio pushing the controls on the desk and all I could see him doing was bring up bass lines and bringing up the high treble at the top end of the guitar line and putting Mick's voice forward. Bill Wyman was there. He had a great pair of trousers. They were stovepipe trousers – which I was very impressed by because I was very much into clothes. Anyway, so I knocked around with the Stones and used to go to their early gigs. In fact, I lived with Mick and Keith for a little while in Mapesbury Road in South West Hampstead. It was really Cricklewood bordering on Kilburn[64]. You can't get much worse than that as a bedsitter land because nothing happens out there I can tell you. I sussed out what the Stones were about, and their appeal, and I saw for the first time in my life all those little girls screaming at them. They were doing their R & B, not Booker T[65] or the Georgie Fame[66] trip, but just really good R & B. There was Mick up there in his Ghillie jacket. Mine cost $150. His cost him £30 but the collar wasn't right anyway. So, I lived with Mick and Keith, and they were great, and I sussed it out. Andrew was making fortunes then. I was doing publicity just for people I liked, like Chuck Berry, which is rather a long-winded way of saying that I suddenly thought, "Wow!" I was going down to this mod club most nights of the week with 10 bob in my pocket, I was on Drinamyl which made me feel good and then I'd have a pint of

63 Meaden has conflated two memories. The session he is referring to is likely to be one on August 8 1963 when the Stones recorded Chuck Berry's 'Bye Bye Johnny', Barrett Strong's 'Money' and Arthur Alexander's 'You Better Move On' for their first EP. 'Come On' was recorded at Olympic Sound Studios, then near Marble Arch, on May 2 and entered the *NME* charts on August 2, hence Meaden's confusion. When 'Come On' was recorded he was still in Madrid.
64 The flat, at 33 Mapesbury Road, NW2, was closer to Willesden and Brondesbury than it was to Kilburn.
65 Booker T. Jones was the keyboard player who led Booker T. and The M.G.'s, an instrumental soul band from Memphis. They were best known for their 1962 hit 'Green Onions' and later became the house band for such Stax/Volt touring acts as Sam and Dave, Otis Redding and Arthur Conley.
66 Georgie Fame (1943 -) was born Clive Powell and played jazz influenced blues on a Hammond organ with backing by his band The Blue Flames. He was a regular at The Flamingo and benefited from music passed on to him by American servicemen and West Indian immigrants.

cider on top of that which made me feel even better and I was grooving on 'til it was time to go home and then when it came to the weekend I was going to *Ready Steady Go!* and after that going over to the West End, grooving around for a bit, taking a few pills so it would start hitting it at around 8 'o' clock and just dancing around, going over to a pub and then listening to Guy Stevens playing a few records. I was having a good life. Now, I was thinking, all the mods were not identifying with groups like The Animals or the Stones. The Stones appeared at The Scene club, but they didn't have the mod identification factor.

The Stones played The Scene?

Yeh, oh yeh. I used to go down there with Brian Jones who was a very close friend of mine. I was close to Mick and Keith via Andrew, in so much as he was their manager then and he was my very, very close friend from the age of 19 or 20. We had been very close. We'd had companies together and all sorts of things. Mick and Keith were much cooler than that. Brian liked to come down there. He would come out with me because he liked to groove around, and he would come down with his snakeskin boots, his Regency stuff and his high scarf. He'd come down to The Scene and I'd be wearing Ivy League, which was Canadian-cum-American Esquire[67] jackets that were soft and comfortable with natural shoulder lines and all that - very comfortable clothes. I'd be grooving about in my desert boots and having a bop around, listening to the music and Brian was a top superstar, number one, coming up fast but he felt out of place in The Scene club. He felt that. It was so cliquish. The mods were so highly identified with themselves. He was culture, actually like a culture dish or a culture bed in a hospital where they make penicillin – something very pure, developing. And when the hippest, heaviest outfit in the world, which was the Stones, didn't fit in – that meant something was

---

67 Mods enjoyed the American magazine *Esquire* because of the adverts and fashion spreads. There was no UK edition of the magazine at the time.

wrong somewhere. Now I identified with the mods because it was total freedom. It was going to a place where you could stay for three days on the straight because of the strength of a few pills. I was going down on a Friday night and stacking it out until Sunday morning[68] when I'd hitch hike home and get picked up by Rick Gunnell[69] coming home from The Flamingo Club which was a different scene altogether, which was US air base men. So, I'd figured out that the mods were my people 'cos I was having a great time; three days of the week straight on, full up of everything you wanted – music, food, pills which gave you everything you needed which was nirvana. It was music, bopping around and having a good time, being private, having a chat with a couple of mates, not too many chicks around to faze you with that competitive trip of fancying other geezers. The mod girls were there just to give that little bit of spice to life because it was an asexual situation.

It really was?

It really was because the Drinamyl, or speed as they call it now. They gave you satisfaction. Old Mick used to sing 'can't get no satisfaction.' Well, you could get that satisfaction on Drinamyl! It wasn't like acid or the things that came later. Mods weren't too heavily into chicks because chicks, you must remember, are emotionally stressful situations for a man. When you're totally free because your sexual drives, your libido, is turned right down low, you no longer have to worry about your dick, you no longer have to worry about pulling a chick and making it because that's what you feel the world made you for. It didn't in fact. It made you perhaps to marry a woman and have children with her, but you didn't need to get too heavily into sex or pulling chicks or 'sorts' as we called them. "Any sorts coming down tonight? Oh, it don't matter anyway. You don't need to

68 The advertised hours for The Scene club in 1964 were 8 pm to 1 am weekdays and 8pm to 3 am on a Saturday night. If you were a member entrance was free during the week and cost five shillings at the weekend.
69 Rick Gunnell (1931-2007) was a club owner, manager and promoter who began putting on music in Soho in the early Fifties. His best-known club was The Flamingo in Wardour Street. In 1968 he opened the Bag O' Nails in Kingly Street which attracted pop stars after hours.

bother when they come down" was the trip, man. There were three of them dancing over in the corner.

Were the mod girls also not into sex?

They were likewise not into sex. They were very matriarchal. They would be looked after and protected. There would be three girls dancing together. There is a famous picture of them dancing a dance called the block. When you'd taken pills you were what was known as 'blocked.' I don't know where it came from. I know amphetamines block out your nerve ends after about a year[70]. The aphorisms and words of the mod language are very succinct and very powerful. Women were just the people who danced over in the corner by the speakers, up front, the thin ones they had in those days. The Who had the biggest ones of all and that was much better. Before that it would be powerful records coming through speakers like you would hear at fairgrounds. It was a concrete floor and the sound would bounce up off the floor and hit you in the ear holes BOOMP! You'd be bopping away and grooving because it didn't matter what you did. The whole beauty of amphetamine was that you were in control. You were in control of your situation; you were in control of your voice. If you felt like speaking, you spoke. If you didn't feel like speaking, you didn't speak. You were totally in control. You didn't 'have to' do things. You were free. You were absolutely free from libido, from sexual drives, because there was no competition. The only competition involved was in having a good time, looking good, bopping round and being nice to the other geezers as well.

So, it was bliss?

It was bliss. Cocaine they say is bliss these days but it's not bliss like a bit of speed in you, a couple of pints of cider maybe, down there bopping round from Friday night though until Sunday morning. Say no more! I think that when you eliminate sex,

---

70 In a medical sense 'blocked' means; "To interrupt or obstruct the proper function of (a psychological process), especially by the use of drugs."

sexual competition, from man's games, his games of existence or existing, you live a life of Riley. When it comes to reproducing the race, then you get into women, you know, but once you let women into your life they take over everything. They take over like a spider's web and it gets cobwebby and it gets tacky and we have a free man, a freeman of the city, on a couple of doobs, a couple of pints of cider, a lot of Tony Clarke records, 'Daddy Rolling Stone' by Derek Martin[71] and a few other things.

What happened to your sex drive during the week?

Because you didn't make it at the weekend you didn't bother about it in the week because you had to work in the week. Therefore, you were a totally solo person which is what I think man is supposed to be. You were a solo person. You could live by yourself and live with yourself. You're only made to feel lonely because of guilt. Guilt and the media say that you should link up with a woman and the church says you should link up with a woman and your parents say that eventually you should link up with a girlfriend. You find that masturbation is as much a solace as it is a relief. If you can survive on that, you can survive on anything. It means that you're no longer dependent on other people. You're a free man. A Freman. Mod living or modism is an aphorism for free living, real free living, because you've discarded all values, because you're on a drug that hits you so hard you can feel the rise and the rush coming up. It's very safe. It's made by the government, or I should say that it's licensed by the government, and they still supply it through certain doctors. I don't take it myself any more because I'm not into that scene too heavily, but I still enjoy it very much when I do take it because I'm the only person in London who goes down and asks for 60 Dexedrine from his doctor and his doctor says, "Yeh. Do you want any sleeping pills to go with it, or any Valium?"

Is mod life purely experiential?

71 Derek Martin (1938 -) released 'Daddy Rolling Stone' in 1963 on the Crackerjack label. It was a cover of a song written by Otis Blackwell, the author of such rock and roll classics as 'Great Balls of Fire,' 'All Shook Up' and 'Don't Be Cruel.' The Who played the song on the American TV programme *Shindig* in 1965.

It's discovering new life so strongly because there you are a free man unlimited by time and space. No longer does sleep mean anything and no longer do hours mean anything. Here's a club which caters for your need - The Scene club. You're out there on the dance floor by yourself, hogging the limelight, because that's all a man does when he dances. I don't know about women. I think women feel the same as well. But if a man dances around, or just bops around to a record, doing the 'The Monkey Time'[72] or stuff like that because someone else is doing it and little Mickey Tenner is out there doing it as well. Everyone's out on the pills and you're doing it just to records. You're free. You're free of time and space inasmuch as the only space involved is the space in your head and that's really spaced when you're on speed. There's just a little bit of barbiturate in Drinamyl to take the edge off the nervousness of the amphetamine and then alcohol on top of that combines to make you so comfortably lush – not lush in the drink sense but lush in the comfortable, groovy sense.

If you took away the dancing and the music, what would be left?

If you took away the dancing, you'd have the West End.

Just moving around the city?

Grooving around on a Saturday morning after a long night out, all Friday night. You have to remember, you're bunged out on your ear hole at about six in the morning and it's probably cold, grey and dry. I must say, 'lush' is not the right word but it's not the wrong word either. Lush, not in the drink sense, but in the sense that it's so comfortable, so groovy, so clean and so fresh, that it's lush like lush vegetation. The word 'lush' – it's not sloppy drunk because you never get drunk when you're a mod. You have drinks. You drink cider or you drink beer with your pills – your Drinamyl, Purple Hearts, Dexies, blues, Frenchies or whatever you can get your hands on. "Please lay a doobrie on me! Got any Licorice All Sorts? Got any Dolly Mixtures[73]?" Anyway,

72 'The Monkey Time' by Major Lance was released on Edsel in 1963.
73 Dolly Mixtures and Liquorice All Sorts were small sweets made by Geo. Bassett & Co (now part of Cadbury).

so you go back to the West End on a cold Saturday morning and you go to some café which sells you French coffee, black coffee, you've got your scarf round your neck with a single mod twist, or double if you're flash. In my case I'd be bombing around with Phil the Greek who'd have a shotgun in his Zodiac, around the back there, and you'd sit around until the shops started opening up on Saturday morning and you'd groove around, go sit in a pub or look around Cecil Gee's, although mainly you'd go to Austin's[74] and get yourself an Arrow shirt[75] with button down collars and a button at the back of the collar as well and then you'd groove around with your new buy, your new purchase and it'd be a groove. You have paradise on hand. In most mod language 200 blues in your inside pocket of your Tonik[76] jacket and you'd have sustained relief from the world. Sustained release comes when you go down to The Scene club which is so cliquish and so private and so mod. You must remember we all live so much inside our heads that it becomes private. You're doing all the things you've always wanted to do. You're free of your parents, free of your friends who are not mods, you're free of girlfriends and people who drag on your time and want to go to the pictures or something like that. When you go down The Scene club you're free.

But what was life like when you weren't on the pills? You have to come down again.

You've got to sustain it for the weekend. That's all.

With dancing and music?

Not necessarily.

Could you have the same thing if you were watching television with your parents?

No! No way. This is why The Scene club was so strong and the mod movement, the revolution.

Opposite: The Scene club was "so cliquish and so private and so mod". Mickey Tenner can be seen at centre, right

74 Austin's was a clothing shop on Shaftesbury Avenue that specialised in American imports.
75 Arrow was an American brand of shirt made by Cluett, Peabody & Co.
76 Tonik was a cloth weave created by Dormeuil in 1957 that used two colours to produce a mohair-type sheen. The name is a company copyright and is often misspelt Tonic.

This is what I'm saying. Take away the dancing and the music and there would be no point in taking the pills?

No. You'd be a hippy then. A hippy doesn't depend on music as much as a mod does. A mod needs hard, fast and loose new wave R&B which is the old Curtis Mayfield stuff, Major Lance, Derek Martin, all that heavy air base R&B stuff which we used to play down The Scene club. What happened was that Sandra[77] was a disc jockey there and she had a spade boyfriend from an air base and he used to lay these R&B soul records on her. She used to go out with all these spades from the air bases. You know what I mean? They were a little bit different. They were not Stateside so they only carried around the finest records with them and that's what they'd play in soul clubs on the air bases and that's what they would play down The Scene club. Guy Stevens used to play them, and old Sandra used to play the real good stuff. I used to go down there with John Paul Jones[78], who is now of Led Zeppelin fame, who'd play his bass records and stuff like that. It was a life that was so idyllic, so beautifully compact. You gotta remember that a mod is compact. He's a moving unit with no possessions apart from his togs, the clothes he's got on him.

The pills are directly tied to the activities?

Yeh. That gives you the freedom. That gives you sustaining power. Imagine having a party that starts Friday night and doesn't end until Sunday morning, and you can have it any time you want it. If you want to start it on Wednesday night, you can, although you'd be a bit worn out by Thursday evening, but you could kip for a bit in a park or go back home to Mum's place, have a kip and then come back up to town. You'd get a few blisters on your tongue. You don't have to talk too much. You don't have to do much at all. Just have a good time and feel good.

What was your attitude towards your job?

77 Sandra Blackstone nee Lane (1939 - ??) was born in Portsmouth, Hampshire.
78 John Paul Jones was a noted session musician before joining Led Zeppelin. In Andrew Oldham's book *Stoned* he is quoted as saying; "He (Meaden) was exciting, knew where all the bands were; he knew what was good to see…The Face, yeh. That was Peter."

I used to work at an advertising agency when I first started being a mod and then I split from that and I was a graphic designer.

Did you think it was a cop-out to have a job?

Well, it used to buy my clothes. Then I became a publicist.

Did you use society?

No. I didn't use society. I became a publicist. I used to do Chuck Berry's publicity[79].

But you said that a mod takes what is there.

Yes. He takes what is there.

But a hippie doesn't?

A hippie doesn't do anything except vegetate and groove off of various identification points such as religions which are very easy to identify with because that's all they are. They are identification points. They are specially sculpted and carved by man to appeal to other men in the most delicious, sensuous or aesthetic way – whichever way you want to do it. I mean there's Buddhism, Lao-Tse, Maoism, Christianity, Judaism, Hinduism, Lafayette Ron Hubbard[80]. You can pick up on the Process people[81]. You can pick up on Charles Manson if you want to. I personally happened to pick up on the mods.

So, mod-ism is like a religion?

Yeh. I made an album by Jimmy James and The Vagabonds, which was the real purist mod band, a band that played R&B with saxes, the drums and the organ. I managed them for three and a half years and Jimmy James had the best voice there was around, the best I'd ever heard. That was the purist thing as far as mod music was concerned.

The musicians were black, right?

Yeh. They were coloured.

There was still no white band that represented the mods?

Yeh. The Who.

---

79 Chuck Berry mentions Meaden in his autobiography but misspells his name as Pete Meade.
80 Lafayette Ronald Hubbard (1911-1986) was a science fiction writer and the founder of a self-help system that became the religion of Scientology.
81 The Process was a Californian cult of the late Sixties that taught that God and the Devil were one.

But before The Who?

No there wasn't. There was old Chris Farlowe[82] doing mod stuff but they weren't mods. They didn't look like mods. Jimmy James and The Vagabonds was the escape. It was the black release, what I call the black release. I made an album with them called The New Religion[83] and it started off with: "Yeh, and the faces would dig the rapport and the faces would jump on stage and everyone would have a good time because it was Vags party time – Vagabonds party time." That's what having a mod society is all about. It's about having a continuous party, sustaining it for as long as you can without doing too much damage to your body, but taking it right out on the rim. Old Dylan was out there on the rim. He lived out on the rim and he wrote about the rim. When you're out on the rim, right out on the edge there, as far out as you can go, far out on Ridgeville, it's really Turn-It-Down City because when you get that far out you know you gotta cool it a bit because it starts getting into nerve ends. Modism was a way of life that was so succinctly, beautifully British. It was so direct down to communications because it's a fast communication city is Britain because Britain is nothing more than a city with London and a few other cities. It's the City of Britain, you know. As I say, I used to travel around with the Vagabonds and we had this album called The New Religion and it was the finest in new wave R&B that you can imagine.

This was before The Who?

No. This is after The Who. I went into real modism after that. Real purism. Like...I don't know what hedonism means but...

It means living for pleasure.

No. I was working very hard. I was living for pleasure in the sense that I liked to have a good time every night of the week. I made my

Opposite: According to Peter Meaden, Bob Dylan was "out there on the rim." In 1966 he was also out there in Carnaby Street buying the latest in mod jackets, shirts, and trousers

82 Chris Farlowe (1940 -   ) was one of the few white singers whose records were enjoyed by mods. He had his biggest success with singles of Andrew Oldham's Immediate label. His best-known hit was 'Out of Time' (written by Keith Richards and Mick Jagger) which made the number one spot in 1966.
83 'The New Religion' by Jimmy James and The Vagabonds (1966).

own personal discotheque in the form of seven or eight live guys on stage with saxes and trumpets. They were not doing Georgie Fame R&B but doing real new wave R&B.

Did you feel there was a need for a group like The Who?

There was a need for The Who, exactly, coming back to that. I had this lovely life going on for me which was having a good time, enjoying myself. Other people didn't bother me, and I didn't bother them. Nobody bothered anybody else but smiled at each other, not in a hippy way, but a mod suss smile like "I like the suit man. Great. I like the top button just done up there. Groove on." Not too heavy. Even Brian Jones didn't fit in down at The Scene club. In the old way it was 'hep', then it became 'hip'. It's hip to live life out on the wire, that far out in Stoned City which is London late night. Nobody wants you, unless you got bread to pay for it. You could go down The Scene club and have nirvana, have a haven, have a port, for being a ram which is just thrusting ahead and having a good time. You used to see those three or four mod kids in Tonik jackets, Levi jeans just turned up one turn, desert boots or Hush Puppies and they'd lean forward, they'd have the energy of leaning forward as they walked up Great Windmill Street or down Shaftesbury Avenue. They'd be talking and they'd have their crews on – French crew cuts – or they'd be wearing a cycling jacket, a bicycling jacket with a number on the back or a plain white one or a black one. I thought, ah, this is it. We have to have a focus. So, I was thinking about, there are no other bands who are doing this as pure as I am because I'm really the Detail Man. I really am the Detail Man. When it comes to detail, that's my trip. I thought, I've gotta have a band. I've gotta make the focus because even though the Stones have played down there [84] and The Animals have played down there, and Chuck Berry comes down who was a personal friend of mine who I've idolised ever since I heard 'You Can't Catch Me'[85]. That's what modism is. "You can't catch me." "I just want to evade you

84 The Rolling Stones started a Thursday night residency at The Scene club in June 1963 after the Crawdaddy Club at the Station Hotel in Richmond was closed down. Brian Jones contacted Ronan O'Rahilly.
85 'You Can't Catch Me' by Chuck Berry was released in 1956.

because I don't want to get hurt and I want to live good as well".
I figured, I gotta get a band together to be so perfect, so just right
on, so perfectly spot on. Then Phil the Greek who had a dark blue
Zodiac[86] with a big hump back, dark blue mohair suits with the
middle button done up - he even had the nerve to wear Anello &
Davide[87] boots with his blue suit – a blue Jacques Fath[88] heavy
silk tie with stripes (very tasteful), a big gold tie clip, a couple of
big gold rings on his right hand, another big gold ring on his left
hand, and the heaviest French crew you've ever seen. I used to
heave around with him in his Zodiac 'cos all the other kids were
into scooters – I preferred the motor to be perfectly honest – and
he used to carry a sawn-off shotgun in his car. He used to load
up the cartridges with paper, not lead shot. The paper would tear
your face off! I can't think of anything more vicious than that. It
wouldn't harm you. It would just take your face off. Anyway, I'd
go down to The Scene club with him and he'd say, "Listen Pete.
I've got a band here. There's a fellow – anyway, you come along
with me and have a listen." So, we went to Jack's and I knew Jack
in a vague way. I had my haircut and Jack says, "There's a friend
of mine called Helmut Gorden who's a very powerful doorknob
maker and they have this band. You're in the pop business aren't
you?' I said, "Yeh. I know the Stones and I used to live with the
Stones as a matter of fact. I lived with Mick and Keith for a while.
I'd go to their gigs. Why?" He said, "They're a good band. Do you
reckon you could manage them?" I said, "I expect so. I don't know.
What are you talking about?" Then I thought, "Ah. Could this be
the band that I could make into the mod trip? Could they be my
focus, my focal point for the good life?" It needed a focus because
when you've got a good life going you've got to sustain it. You
can't let it groove on for the sake of it and then let it wear out

86 The Ford Zodiac, first manufactured in 1956, was the company's largest and plushest passenger car to be produced as Dagenham.
87 Anello & Davide, established in 1922 by Italian immigrant brothers, had a shop in Charing Cross Road. They pioneered the boots with elastic or zipped sides that became popularised as 'Beatle boots' or 'Chelsea boots.'
88 Jacques Fath (1912-1954) was a French designer. After his death the company concentrated on perfumes, gloves, hosiery and other accessories.

Steve Turner interviewing Peter Meaden, Shepherd Street, London, May 12, 1975

because the duration has run out and people are getting tired and bored. You need regeneration in everything. You've got to have energy put into things. So, I went down with Jack who introduced me to Helmut Gorden and he introduced me to another geezer who was a fellow called Bob Druce, an agent who ran a little circuit of half a dozen or so pubs where he'd put his bands in[89]. I asked whether he had a contract on The Who or something. I don't know whether he ever did or not. Bob Druce was the hard man in this situation. He was a man who was just into booking a group which he knew were successful into his clubs. Then he could more or less guarantee to keep them working in his six clubs, his little circuit which was definitely tailored to 'kid pub' situations. He knew where his market was, and he was just trying to heighten it up a little bit. He said, "Why don't you come in and help us out? Get this group. They're a very good group called The Detours. Do you think you could do something like that, you being in the pop business and knowing The Rolling Stones and Chuck Berry and all those people? Using your knowledge from The Rolling Stones do you think you could make a super group out of them? We'll give you fifty quid to start off. "So, I said, "Fifty quid? That's a lot of money isn't it!!" Nice one. I'm known as the low budget man. No one ever pays me. Not even Robert Stigwood[90]. Don Arden[91] certainly doesn't and Rick Gunnell is very difficult when it comes to bread. I was doing Georgie Fame's publicity. I thought, great, here we go again. Another low-budget number. I was knocking around with Peter and Gordon[92] before that and I

89 Gorden and Druce had formed a company Gorden-Druce Enterprises Limited.
91 Robert Stigwood (b 1934) was an Australian entrepreneur best known for managing the likes of The Bee Gees and Eric Clapton and producing the movies *Grease* and *Saturday Night Fever*. Coincidentally *Saturday Night Fever* was based on an article by British writer Nik Cohn which appeared in *New York* magazine. Purporting to be about the Seventies disco phenomenon in Brooklyn he later revealed that much of it was based on his memory of the mod era in London's Shepherd's Bush. Cohn was a huge fan of The Who and the inspiration behind the song 'Pinball Wizard.'
91 Don Arden (1926-2007) was a legendary manager who started out in the mid-Fifties. He managed The Small Faces and later Black Sabbath. He was noted for his intimidating behavior. His daughter, Sharon, married Ozzy Osbourne and is mother to Kelly and Jack.
92 Peter Asher (1944 -   ) and Gordon Waller (1945-2009) formed the singing duo Peter and Gordon in 1962. In 1964 they became part of the 'British invasion' of America. Asher's family home in Wimpole Street, London W1, which he shared with his actor sister Jane, became a meeting point for important figures on the London 'underground' scene including John Lennon Paul McCartney, John Dunbar and Barry Miles.

was Bob Dylan's first publicist in this country[93]. I knew where it was at. I handled Tommy Tucker[94] and was also publicist for Chuck Berry, The Crystals and The Rolling Stones. So, all right squire, you're going to give me fifty quid are you? So, I'll get fifty quid and I'll put The Who together.

How did you spend the money?

I spent it on clothes, of course. Because togs are the only thing which keep a mod together. Outside of that he's a bag of protoplasm, smashed out on the street with no one giving a damn for him. With his togs and a few pills inside him he's God. He's as much God as you and I are. He's as heavy as you want him to be and he's heavy. Yeh, so I was asked to make a super group with £50.

Who gave you the £50?

Helmut Gorden. I said, "We'll make a record too. We'll do it with Fontana[95] because you'll make a deal there quick. No strings attached, just a record out. I'll do all the work on it. I'll do the publicity. I'll do the promotion.

Was this £50 a week?

No. Fifty quid. That's all. I'll put the group together. I'll get the clothes, the right togs. It is togs because togs give you self-respect. They've always given people self-respect. Whether people take money away from me or take worldly goods away from me I'd say that I never took trust away from people. I always gave trust and abhorred distrust. So, I met The Who in Goldhawk Road. I think it was at a rehearsal[96].

This was your first meeting?

Yeh. This was the first time I'd met them, and they were all wearing Pierre Cardin leather jackets[97]. They had cropped hair at the back and Beatle cuts in the front. They were called

93 Dylan first came to Britain in November 1962 which was when he met Andrew Oldham.
94 Tommy Tucker (1933-1982) was an American R&B singer who had a 1964 hit with 'Hi-Heel Sneakers'. He toured Britain in October 1964 on a bill with Carl Perkins and The Animals.
95 The Fontana label was a subsidiary of Phillips Records that was set up in 1954.
96 This was probably at the Goldhawk Social Club, 205 Goldhawk Road, a venue in Shepherd's Bush where The Who played many times between June 1963 and December 1965.
97 The leather jackets were designed by Pete Townshend rather than by the French fashion icon Pierre Cardin.

The Detours[98] and they were into John Lee Hooker[99] and early blues styles. Roger was playing the harmonica and I liked that. I thought the harmonica was great. It was fabulous. I didn't do any more than say, "Listen fellows. If you want to come along with me, I've got the plan for making you a master group. Not a supergroup - a mastergroup." I was wearing very groovy clothes at the time – a comfortable three button American jacket with the top button either done up or left undone. I felt comfortable. I knew what I was doing. I knew where the Stones were at and here was a group that was just playing in a Shepherd's Bush rehearsal room and I said to them, "Listen. I have the key to it all. Listen to me. Please be my mates. All I need is for you to talk to me. I don't need much out of people other than that. If we make money on the side, which I know of course we will, that's good, that's groovy. All I need is the friendship capacity of four geezers. I'll lay out to you how you should do it." Now I'm psychic. Pete Townshend said to me last Monday afternoon that I was psychic. He knows where I'm at. Yeh, I'm psychic in so much as I just made you to be friends of mine.

But you also wanted them to be the focal point of modism?

They were my friends. And my best friends were the ones that could be the focal point for the mods. Now my friends were the mods. Now if I could entertain them, if I could lay an entertainment trip on the mods which was so pure and so definitively their groove... I had The Who. I went down to the rehearsal rooms and I said, "We gotta get some clothes together and you gotta do this certain sound of music which I'm calling new wave R&B which is like R&B, funk, plus soul, plus grooving off the walls, cos that's what you have to do when you're high, you know? And I want to call you not The Detours but The High Numbers. The High Numbers because we're all into pills, into a

98 The name changes can be confusing. The Detours, Roger's group, had existed sine 1957. They became The Who in February 1964 after discovering a Pye recording act was known as Johnny Devlin and The Detours. Pete Towshend's art school friend Richard Barnes came up with the new name. Then, under Meaden's guidance they became The High Numbers before reverting back to The Who.
99 John Lee Hooker (1917-2001) was a blues singer born in Mississippi.

bit of pot, into doing these things, and when we're hip we've got to be this hip. We're gonna be called The High Numbers because, I said, certain strange things are happening to me. Certain high things were coming to me in so much as I was meeting these guys who didn't look exactly like mods, but I'd make them the best that I could. I accepted them as mates and they were the best mates that any geezer could possibly wish for. I told them that I was gonna make them so superb that they could stand up in any conflict, any conflagration, any problem situation, and be the best mates that anyone could possibly have. I said "I will make you mates cos this is where mods are at. If we're gonna be best mates you're gonna be divided by an eighteen-inch high stage at The Scene club and that's the only division there'll be between my mates." So, I said, "You be private and you do these things for me." I remember we went out and we spent the fifty quid. For £30 we bought a jacket. The rest went on boxing boots, which Pete paid a bit towards.

Real boxing boots?

Yeh. Boxing boots. I wrote about them on the handout[100] – "Ivy League jacket, white buckskin shoes." I bought Roger a pair of Hush Puppies. They were brown and I painted the back dark blue and the front white. They were the "two tone brogues" which I mentioned in 'Zoot Suit.' I put all that together. He had an Ivy League jacket with actual 'side vents five inches long' that cost about £30 in Austins. They were into buying their own Arrow shirts with button down collars, comfortable. Oxford Club shirts, you know? I kitted them out. I spent £30 on the jacket. The rest of it we chipped in together. We went into Austins. I had convinced Pete. He was identifying very heavily with the mod trip because I'd said to them, "Listen fellows. Let's go down to The Scene club."

Was this their first contact with mods?

---

100 This refers to Meaden's publicity handout for the 'I Am The Face/Zoot Suit' single which he both wrote and designed.

They were singing Beatles songs, Dylan songs, blues songs, John Lee Hooker. I was easy riding into a situation where they would see that I'd spent time with the Stones who were the successful hip group at the time. You can't deny the Stones where they're at, right? I said, "Where's that at man? We'll top this." I said it as casually as that I said, "Listen to me man." This was to Pete and Roger. They had an older drummer at the time[101] and Pete said, "I'm not too keen on him. What do you think of the new fellow that's just come up? He's going to try it out." I was walking down Knightsbridge with Keith Moon and I said, "Look. I'll speak to Pete Townshend, my mate. He's my mate. It's all right. I'll talk to him and I think you're in because you look a bit better."

Keith told me that he got himself into the group.

He did, yeh. He rowed himself in, but I asked Pete to come in and we brought Keith in for the session for 'I'm The Face' and 'Zoot Suit.' [102]

Did you take them to The Scene club to check it out?

I took them down the Scene. Went down there, had a groove around, and I said, "Look. You can't go wrong. It's just a market but it's not just a market. I'm enjoying it, you can get off on it, I can get off on it. Why don't we become the focal point of this brand-new field of music and lifestyle and not get too uptight about it?" We didn't want to stop enjoying ourselves which is what you can get into when you get into religion. It's all very well getting into religion but when you start going over the mark which is like identifying with every tribute and tribulation the religion wants to lay on you. Just enjoy it, on the line. That's what is known as the bottom line in business terms. Getting down to the bottom line is saying to yourself, "Where's that at? What's happening? What do I need? I've got this and I've got that, I haven't got this or I haven't got that. What precisely do I need?" Mod is another

Opposite: Peter arranged for Eve Bowen to photograph The High Numbers at Picadilly Circus wearing their newly acquired mod togs

101 This was Doug Sandom (1930 - 2019).
102 The recording session took place at Philips' studio in Stanhope Place, London W1, in June 1964.

aphorism for precision in life. It's precision outside the regulated rules of society. I said, "Listen fellows. You come down to The Scene club" and they came down. I checked out the other day. I thought I was the first person to give Pete Townshend Drinamyl. He gave me my first tab of acid. But on Monday he said, when I phoned him up, that he had taken pills before. What happened was I said, "We've got to do this record and we've got to do it fast. I haven't got much money and I haven't got much time. I don't know who's supposed to be manager, but I think I'm supposed to be managing now that I'm taking over responsibility for this." I took over responsibility for The Who. That's what I'm saying.

You financed them yourself?

No. I had fifty quid.

But that didn't last long.

No, it didn't. We had to spend our own money. I chipped in.

You financed them yourself?

Yeh. I spent all night making Roger's shows, the two-tone brogues, from the famous Who song which I says; 'I wear two-tone brogues.'

What was their reaction to the mod scene?

Well, we natched[103] in naturally. We natched in on a scene which is so natural to natch in on. What I'm trying to say is we synchronised with the situation where you couldn't go wrong. Brian Jones felt uptight because he didn't fit in with his snakeskin boots when everyone was wearing desert boots. Chuck Berry felt uptight because he felt the vibe that he was a spade. The Animals were just playing raucous rock and roll. None of them were tailor-made. When you're a mod you want things tailor-made. The jacket has to be tailor-made. The shoes have to be just right. Everything has to be just right. The detail. It's like custom-built and then you shoot the man if his shoulder pads are wrong, you know?[104] You just don't go back. You don't

103 He appears to have coined this verb.
104 Here 'the man' appears to be a tailor who gets his measurements wrong rather than a mod who doesn't look right. 'You don't go back. You don't even accept the jacket' is his anticipated response to bad tailoring.

even accept the jacket. You look at him and you feel ill 'cause he's done something wrong. There's something so precious to you that somebody else has abused.

I know what your reaction was and what you wanted to do with The Who but what was their reaction to your idea?

Well Pete identified immediately. We went down to Austin's to get the jacket [for Roger] made. Which was the one with side vents five inches long. The famous side vents, out of 'I Am the Face'. It was a seersucker jacket with three buttons, Ivy League style far apart, and Roger used to wear black or dark blue trousers to go with the two-tone shoes. We went into Austin's to get the jacket and Keith Moon was messing around and Pete Townshend spat on Keith in the shop and it upset the tailor and because of that he made the shoulders wrong on the jacket[105].

Where did you get the name The High Numbers?

I used to lie in bed at my parents' house in Edmonton, just opposite the Regal Cinema[106], and I'd think, "If I can get a mod group together that would just about solve the problem, I wouldn't have the problem of Mick, Keith and the boys doing their groupie thing with all them girls cheering." I was thinking, "What about the fellows? There has to be something for the fellows." I liked Mick. I thought Mick was great. I liked Keith. I thought he was special. And I knocked around with Brian. But they weren't actually into my scene which was The Scene club, which is mods. They had little girls screaming at them in Woking and places like that. They'd do their early R&B stuff. But my vision is to hip in with the mods and get a private army going and maybe we can make something out of it I knew I was a taste-master of all time. I'm not trying to be boastful, but I know that being a taste-master you know what's gonna happen. You're a marketing man. When you're living your own life, everything

---

105 See previous footnote.
106 The art deco Regal was on the corner of Fore Street and Silver Street. It opened in 1934, became a discotheque in the Seventies and then a bingo club before being demolished in 1985. It could seat almost 3,000 patrons and had capacity for an extra 1,000 standing. The Beatles and Frank Sinatra played there and it was where Cliff Richard came in 1957 to see Bill Haley and the Comets on their first tour of Britain.

is marketing. When you're living your own life, just having a good time, you're selling the ultimate product which is 'Have a good time 'cos it's all right'– the old Impressions song, right? So, I went down with The Who and we rehearsed in various scout halls, church halls and stuff. I was later to do this with Hawkwind. I said, "Peter. I want a name which is zappy enough." I used to lie in my single bed and think, "A name. A name. The W. H. O. – World Health Organisation. Well that's alright but it's too abstract, too ethereal, too airy-fairy to connect with me. It's called the World Health Organisation and that's good, but I need a name that is adaptable that is going to sustain the length of time. It's got to be more than a six-month name or a year name."[107] Remember, R&B was starting to come up. There was Manfred Mann and the Stones. The Beatles were up there. Pete used to say, "We do a few Beatles numbers as well." I'd say, "I like the R&B numbers, but I don't like The Beatles' numbers because The Beatles are doing them, and they wrote them." On the original brochure, asking about their heights I said, "John Entwistle and Pete Townshend are five feet eleven and a half," which is exactly my height. I put this brochure together which was the total mod aphorism – which is a pithy saying for what it's all about. I put The Who together and in the brochure with no help from their so-called manager. I was asked to become their manager. I was manager of The Who and I put it together and I said whatever there was to say about the mods and what The Who were all about and I said it in as pithy and aphoristic a way as you can say it. No one would get it tighter than that and that's what I would say right now. Can you turn it [the tape recorder] off?

Why?

Oh, if you want me to talk. I'm getting angry now – well, not angry in the sense of anger – but to say that a realisation is coming upon

Opposite: Pete Townshend on a shopping spree in London's clothing stores and boutiques. According to Roger Daltrey 'Kit and Chris took (Peter Meaden's) ideas and made them bigger'

107 This would have to have taken place between February and June of 1964 when the band was first performing as The Who.

me to say that when I got the suits right and got the cycling jackets just right with the tee shirts underneath and the boxing boots, the Levis with the one inch turn ups so the inner seam just showed out, Pete's Madras jacket[108] was right on with the top button just done up, I went to the Railway Inn [actually the Railway Hotel] at Harrow and Wealdstone[109] and went up to Kit Lambert[110] and said, "Listen man, this is the heaviest group you've ever seen. If you want to give us a gig, give us a gig. Because if you're a promoter (which is what he had told me) give us a gig[111]. I'm hustling for my boys. They're my mates. Whether you like it or not I'm doing my thing here. I've made them this far. I've made them into an identifiable quantity which is all that religion is. I made a new religion out of four people who later became the heaviest group in the world. I did the hard work on that and I came up to you and you told me that you were a promoter and I gave you the hand-out which said "I am the face. Four hip young men from London say I am The Face and wear Zoot Suit. The first authentic mod record." That was my trip. I did that entirely myself, off my own back. No one helped me. No one encouraged me. I laid it on you Kit and I laid it on you Pete and if you can believe that you can believe anything.

Once you'd got the band and introduced it to the mods and their music and clothes, how did you build the audience for The Who?

They were doing Bob Druce's clubs. He was booking them into a few clubs and a few pubs. I said to Pete and Roger, "If you come and listen to this music at The Scene club and see what you feel about it." Roger, you must remember, was the leader then. I brought in Keith because I remember Keith saying that he was introduced

---

108 Madras jackets were lightweight cotton with a fine texture usually with a plaid, striped or checked pattern. Real madras cloth came from Madras, India, now known as Chenai.

109 Harrow & Wealdstone was the name of the station. The possible date of this meeting, suggested by Andy Neill and Matt Kent, in *The Complete Chronicle of The Who*, is July 14 1964. The building burned down in 2000.

110 Kit Lambert (1935-1981) was the son of noted composer Constant Lambert. He was privately educated, went up to Oxford and then did a brief stint in the army before becoming an assistant director on such films as *Guns of Navarone* and *From Russia with Love*.

111 Lambert and his business partner Chris Stamp were actually film makers at the time and Lambert stumbled on the group when he saw clusters of scooters outside the venue and went inside to see what was happening.

to drumming by Dion[112]. He liked 'The Wanderer.' He thought that was great because I liked Norman Petty's drumming on the early Buddy Holly and The Crickets records [sic][113]. It was that continuous drumming sound, you know? It was almost a drone of drums. I'd said to Keith, "I'll get you into The Who. I'll speak to Pete. He's my mate." That happened. Then I said to Pete, "Listen. If you follow my rule of thumb I can get it off on this trip." I took them down to The Scene club and they saw the mods and they started identifying. They started getting into my special things.

All of them?

Well, Peter primarily. That's why I think he spat on Keith Moon in Austin's when we were buying some real mod clothes. Mod clothes are really simple, clean clothes which you can wear any time of the day or night. They're fresh enough to wear on stage. I was saying, "We don't have to be scruffy like the Stones." I was the first one to lay clothes on the Stones and that was pinstripe waistcoats and trousers, pepper and salt trousers and waistcoats with six buttons down the front. Anyway, Pete says "That's great." And I said to Lionel Blake, "Listen Lionel. Can you book in The Who?" He said, "Yes. Tuesday nights. I think Monday nights or Tuesday nights. We could work a residency up here."[114] He said; "How much do you want?" We said £15 and we'll try and work a percentage on the door as well. I didn't know about this. All I knew was that I had to get them established in the West End, because London was glittering, in a way that they would be recognised by the hard-core cult centre, which was the mods who used to hang out in The Scene club. You can't get any more authentic than that. So, I had to give them the golden seal of authenticity. If they could turn on these kids then they could turn on the world because that's what the next

112 'The Wanderer' by Dion was released in 1961.
113 Norman Petty was the producer. The drummer was Jerry Allison. He was probably thinking in particular of Allison's performance on 'Peggy Sue' (1957).
114 In an issue dated July 25 1964 *Record Mirror* reported that The High Numbers would be appearing at The Scene club every Wednesday for the next three months. In fact they appear to have played there on five Wednesday nights between July 22 1964 and August 26 1964.

move was. I was well into revolution then. I wasn't quite sure of my end, but I knew that if I got a power base going something could happen. So I took The Who down there every Monday or Tuesday night. It was a residency night for The High Numbers. It wasn't The Who, it was The High Numbers and The High Numbers was high because you were on pills or pot or whatever you wanted to do and you were high because you were eighteen inches above the floor, the height on the stage at The Scene club, and you were a number because a number was one of the people who came in and was of the people. A number is like a cloakroom ticket. One of the numbers, you know? You put the two words together – high numbers – this was my meditation in bed at Cuthbert Road in Edmonton, N18. I used to think "High numbers? The High Numbers. Numbers – that's the trip." Strange things were happening to me even then. Paranormal phenomena. Time shifts. All sorts of strange things. That's what it is. When you're that high, high numbers start happening to you. It's nothing to do with, as Chris Stamp[115] said, 'top twentyism.' It was nothing to do with top twentyism. It was the hippest name I'd ever heard of. If you want to getter hipper than that I'll tell you how hip I am. I wrote a song called 'Zoot Suit' which starts off: 'I'm the hippest number in town' but Roger sings it 'I'm the hippiest number in town'. Now the song should go 'I'm the hippest number in town.' And I am the hippest number in town, and I was the hippest number in town then. This isn't a plea for sanity it's just to say that I know where I'm at, I know where my thoughts have been, I know that pop art later on dragged off a lot of the froth of my revolution which I was trying to do then when I was in my mid twenties. In fact, I was 23 years old – 22-23 years old – and modism was my dream, it was having the big turn-on. And I like to say that I call myself a (indecipherable) but it's nothing more than a name which is facetious enough to breakthrough on

115 Chris Stamp (1942-2012) eventual co-manager of The Who along with Kit Lambert, was raised in Plaistow, East London, and was brother of the actor Terence Stamp.

RAILWAY HOTEL
AND
LOUNGE

The Railway Hotel, Harrow and Wealdstone, where Peter introduced Kit Lambert to The High Numbers. This image appeared on the sleeve of The Who's Meaty, Beaty Big Bouncy

whatever front I feel like breaking through on at any particular moment. As long as I am in control of my body, I am in control of my mind, and The Who was my dream. I'm Hard Dreamer of the Thought Patrol, and if that sounds crazy, read on trucker, cos it gets crazier. If you can figure that out of Hard Dreamer and the Thought Patrol came The Who, which were The High Numbers, and that's my pet name for them, and it will remain my pet name for them. They're now the heaviest group, the heaviest stage group in the world; in the world, of the world.

You got them the residency at the Scene. What other gigs were they doing?

They were doing Bob Druce's numbers around in the mod circuit.

There was a mod circuit already in existence?

No. There wasn't a mod circuit. He had a few pubs which I turned into a mod circuit in as much as they were London pubs, around London, and anyone with one eye closed could see how heavy you can get if you got a new market starting up and you've got kids who can actually go in their local vicinity to see a group then naturally they are going to identify with what that group is doing if the freedom implied by what being a mod means is all there. Naturally they're gonna go along to that club and naturally 500 more are going to go along to that club.

When did you write 'I Am the Face'?

I wrote it one morning in early 1964. It came from Guy Stevens' record collection. I thought the record had actually come from Mick Jagger and Keith Richards's record collection, but Pete told me it was from Guy Stevens and that jogged my memory. There was a record called I 'Got Love if You Want It' by Slim Harpo[116]. Slim Harpo was an R&B musician who didn't make much money, as far as I've been able to find out. He died some time ago. He used to get paid in wine. Anyway, I took a rhythm track. I can't

116 James Moore, better known as Slim Harpo (1924-1970) was born in Louisiana. 'Got Love if You Want It' was the B side of his first single 'I'm a King Bee' and was released in 1957.

hold a tune in my head. I can if I've got a good strong tune. I can hold a good strong tune and I can write a song, a lyric that was custom built. You must remember, everything was so tailor-made and custom-built. It's like going to the finest, hippest tailor in town and saying, "I want my suit like this." Well, I did everything like that for The Who. I did it so perfectly I will not allow any denials on any front from anybody. It couldn't have failed because it was so perfectly precision built. It was like going to a tailor and asking for a suit and knowing that the shoulders are going to be just right, the lapels are going to be just hanging right, they're gonna be peaked just high enough to be there, the buttons are going to be just right on, the vent (or vents, perhaps) will be just right on, the trousers are going to be tight enough around the bum and just straight enough done there to go with a pair of shoes you're gonna wear them with, a great pair of desert boots maybe. But, anyway, it's gonna be comfortable enough to be just so right on. It was just right on. What I did with The Who was just right on.

What about 'Zoot Suit?

'Zoot Suit' was the fashion record of all time. It was based on the backing track of 'Country Fool' by The Showmen[117], which was the B-side of 'It Will Stand'.[118] The Showmen are now known as the Chairmen of the Board[119] and 'It Will Stand' is the rock and roll tribute anthem of all time. It had lines like, 'Hear those sax blowing/ Sharper than lightnin' rock and roll... Forever it will stand...Come on boys/Join our clan..." It was a real anthemic song. The B-side was 'Country Fool'. That came from Guy Stevens' record collection. The morning of the session I'd been thinking about the record for some time. I'm always a late deadline worker so the night before the session I wrote down the words, I'd got the melody down, and I'd given the records to

---

117 'It Will Stand' by The Showmen, produced in New Orleans by Allen Toussaint, was first released in 1961 by Minit Records (Minit 632) and then re-released in 1964 by Imperial records (Imperial 66033).
118 Neill and Kent point out that Meaden was wrong here. The melody was taken from 'Misery' by the Dynamics (Big Top Records, 1963). The Dynamics was a Detroit based vocal group.
119 General Norman Johnson left the Showmen in 1968 and became lead singer with The Chairmen of the Board in 1968.

Pete to listen to. They'd heard the melody and the night before the session I just dreamt up the lyrics and wrote them down on speed, on Drinamyl, good old Purple Hearts, which really does clear out your mind.

You wrote new words to this tune?

I wrote new words to both tunes. I'm not a musician.

What were the words to 'Zoot Suit'?

The actual words were 'I'm the hippest number in town/ And I'll tell you why, I'll tell you why' and it goes into 'I wear a zoot suit jacket with side vents five inches long.' It's a great song, man.

Did the mods catch on to it?

Yeh. Of course they did. It was a fashion song. It was a real detail thing.

Did it become a mod anthem?

There were two of them. There was an A and a B-side and I used to go up in the middle of the set when The High Numbers were playing and I'd say "Play the song now. Play the record now." I'd go down to The Scene club and I'd get the record out and I'd ask Sandra to play the record because that was the record that was playing for kids who were out there in their own R&B idiom, with their own feel. So, before The High Numbers went on, and all that week, she'd be playing it. I bought 200-250 records off the record company – off Fontana – to get it into the charts. I used to take them round myself. I worked so hard on that, man.

Did it get into the charts?

No, it didn't, but it got so many (radio) plays that I got £112.[120] I don't know how many pence you got for each play but there were quite a few plays. It was nothing to do with the pirate ships although Mickey Tenner gave it a few plays on Caroline.

Pete Townshend wasn't writing songs at this time?

No, he wasn't.

[120] 'I am the Face' backed with 'Zoot Suit' was released on July 3 1964. It's said to have only sold 500 copies. Both songs were later used on the *Quadrophenia* movie soundtrack album (1979).

Opposite: 'I Am The Face' was inspired by Slim Harpo's 'Got Love If You Want It' which Peter Meaden found in Guy Stevens record collection

What sort of music was The High Numbers playing?

The Detours had been an R&B band.

So, they played no original material at all?

No. They were playing a little bit of Bob Dylan, but mostly Beatles' records and R&B.

But the mods didn't like Beatles records very much.

They didn't like it, man. They weren't allowed to play there. The Who wasn't a mod group before I met them.

But after you met them…

After I met them I said, "We've got to play mod music", which was new wave R&B, all the time, man. Classics you've never heard of; 'Ain't Love Good, Ain't Love Proud,' 'Daddy Rolling Stone,'[121] Motown stuff, 'I Gotta Dance to Keep from Crying' and my favourite one of all, Curtis Mayfield and The Impressions.

Did they play any records themselves?

Records, yes, but it was limited to only one club which was so insanely judicial in its consensus if opinion regarding records. That might sound highfalutin, or whatever you want to call it, but remember, it was very important to be so precisely right on, to get that close to what precision is all about. Precision is being right on, right?

Was The Who becoming the focal point that you wanted them to be? Were the mods starting to talk about them?

Yeh. I got The High Numbers a residency.

Were they taking pills by then?

Yeh, but they didn't worry about it too much. I mean I was pilling up.

Would you have considered them to be real mods?

Now they were, now that I'd changed them, because all mod is, is having self-respect.

Did they wear their mod outfits off-stage as well as on?

Yeh, well I told them to I bought the jacket for Roger. I mean the jacket was the high point of my career, you might say. It was a

---

121 'Daddy Rollin' Stone' was written and released by Otis Blackwell in 1953 but Meaden's favourite version was by Derek Martin, released on Crackerjack Records in 1963.

seersucker jacket, man. I've done a lot of heavy things but that was about the heaviest thing I've ever done.

Did you make them style their hair?

Yeh. Of course I did. I took them down to Jack the barber.

To have French crews?

Well Jack said, "Now I've introduced you to the band" and I said, "Listen Jack. Now you've got to do the haircuts and all."

Was there ever a feeling that you'd made them do all these things as a promotional exercise?[122]

Yeh. I think Roger felt that way.

I think John Entwistle did as well.

I don't know about John.

He told me that he hadn't wanted to wear all these clothes. He walked through a puddle in his boxing boots and the soles fell off.

Yeh, well, I knew I was right on. How can he deny a fact that's smack bang in front of your face? This is where it's at. I'm laying it on you. I can't do anything more. I'm laying it on you as hot and strong as I can. This is where it's at. This is what we're doing. Please do it. We're gonna be a success. We can't help it. Then you can be my mates as well.

I've read interviews with the band from 1964 where they talk about being mods. There must have come a point when they accepted that identity.

Yeh. Mod is a way of life. I went down to Hastings in 1966.

To tackle a few rockers?

There weren't any rockers. There were just mods. That's how overpoweringly successful the whole trip was. There was something like 15,000 mods down there and three rockers in a café. Three! There were two down the road in another café or sitting on their bikes. The mods came down. It was so beautifully succinct. Can you understand the succinctness of the word succinct? I'll get

---

122 I didn't know at the time that Pete Townshend had told *NME* in April 1965; "At this time we had a fanatical mod manager who wanted us all to be the complete mod. But this was a contrived, artificial modness and we wanted to be ourselves."

my dictionary out in a minute.[123]

I know what it means!

It's right on, isn't it? It's succinct. Perfect. It's like getting a button which has got the depressed bit in it where put your thumb and you can feel the depressed bit and then you push the button. You're so confident. You know it's right on. Everything is there to build-in confidence. You know it's right on. I worked so hard.

How did you lose the band?

Well, I wasn't too hip in business. I didn't know there were a lot of thieves about. I'd been called a "pilled-up mod" by a geezer who was nowhere in the music business called Tony Hall[124]. You can quote that as me saying that. The whole point of getting The Who together was because he said to me after going to a Ben. E. King reception, "Get out the reception. You're no longer with the Stones..."[125]

Who said this?

Tony Hall. "And you're a pilled-up mod." Now, I wasn't a 'pilled-up mod'. I'd take two or three a day to keep going. I needed it to stand up to the bullshit artists that there are in the music business. Please quote me on this – bullshit artists I cannot tolerate. They're not the music business and never will be the music business. I abhor them and think they're disgusting, revolting people. All they do is grab money off the cream of the cake. For a man like that, who had no more morals than an alley cat, I would say... Well, that's not exactly true, but I'm getting angry now. He called me 'a pilled-up mod' and I made The Who out of that one phrase. Because I was called a 'pilled-up mod' by a man who has no more respect for the music business than my arsehole. That's Tony Hall. I worked for him later for two-and-a-half years, so I know all about him. I'm a man that speaks the truth. I speak the truth these days.

---

123 The Merriam-Webster dictionary definition of succinct is "Marked by compact precise expression without wasted words." Its origin is in the Latin *succinctus* which meant "having one's clothes gathered up by a belt, tightly wrapped."

124 Despite this outburst, Tony Hall (1928 - 2019) was a well respected figure in the British music industry who at various times worked as an A&R man, producer, radio host, columnist, record plugger, promoter, distributor, publisher and manager.

125 This is likely to have been when Ben. E. King came to Britain in July 1964 and appeared on *Ready Steady Go!*

You didn't lose The Who through that incident though did you?

No, but I made The Who because he called me a 'pilled-up mod.' See, I was the only person. It was the Stones who were respectable because they were on Decca, right? Now The Beatles who were friends of Tony Hall as well and I was a friend of The Rolling Stones and I used to go around to Tony Hall's flat sometimes with the Stones. Andrew Oldham and I used to go around just for a gee-up and a bit of a laugh and there was Tony Hall who was so succinctly aware as far as personalities were concerned couldn't see the biggest personality of all, which was me. I didn't fall out with Andrew, but the Stones became really big and they all drifted away into bigger pastures. I went by myself to a Ben E. King reception and –please put this – Tony Hall told me to piss off out of the reception because I was 'a pilled-up mod'. So, I said, "Thank you man. I'll remember that." Because of him saying that to me I made self-respect part of my jargon again. I said, "If he's gonna call me a pilled-up mod I'll make pilled-up mods the religion or the people of this earth. All a pill is doing is giving you nirvana for a few seconds.

So how did you lose The Who?

I was pushing very hard, getting a lot of photographs and doing a big promotional thing on 'I am the Face' and 'Zoot Suit.' The record was out and getting a lot of plays on the radio because I went around and did all the hard work myself. I was going along to gigs with them and had the promotional handout done which was defending my position and their position as mods. I made them my statement people as far as modism was concerned. Kit Lambert came down that night to the Railway Inn (sic) in Harrow & Wealdstone and he came up to me. He lied to me. He said he was a promoter looking for a band to put into his clubs, so I gave him the hard sell. "This is absolutely where it's at. You cannot fail on this squire." I said, "Listen to me. You can make a lot of money out of this as a promoter if you believe in me because they are of the people. They are the hippest numbers in town. There's no one quite like them. Just look at that queue out there." So, I hard-sold myself right out of a band.

What happened?

Kit came back to me. I tried to get in touch with Pete for a few days after that. Strange things were happening. Pete didn't answer his 'phone or he wasn't at home. I'd been very close to him up until then. Then Roger said, "We're going with this fellow. Let's go and have a drink."

Kit had independently approached the band?

Well Roger was the leader of the band, so Roger and I went and had a drink in a pub in Brewer Street and he said, "Well, listen man. We're gonna get paid £20 a week now, plus our cars. Why don't you have a talk with Kit?" He came out straight with it. He bought a Scotch and I think I bought a Coca Cola and there was nothing more to say about it. Kit then got in touch with me and said, "Let's have lunch." I think it was probably Pete who told him to look after me because I was a very fragile person.

Did you have a contract with the band?

Yeh. I had a contract with them.

Did Kit Lambert buy the contract?

No. I just signed away any rights I had for the first figure he gave me. I figured that if that's what my mates want to do then that's what they have to do Maybe in the future they'll look after me because I need looking after in this life. I need looking after.

Because of your inexperience you sold out?

There was no question about it. I had no opportunity. I was only operating on a mate level. Ask Townshend what that means.

Yet you had a contract?

But that didn't count. Can't you understand that a contract doesn't count when it's on a mate level?

You felt that by sticking to the contract you would lose their friendship?

Yeh. That was more important to me.

Did you continue to be friends after the split?

Yeh. Kit Lambert took me to a restaurant that I'd worked in as a matter of fact, called the Number Four Restaurant in Frith Street. I'd worked there for three days with a friend when I was much

The Who (then The High Numbers) playing at the Railway Hotel in Wealdstone, London, in 1964. Here they were spotted by Chris Stamp and Kit Lambert who soon wrested control of the group from Peter Meaden

younger, learning how to cut onions. I had steak and kidney pie and Kit said, "How much do you want?" and I said, "I don't know how much I want Kit. I don't know what value you'd put on it." I was frightened out of my life because I'd made a monster. I knew it was a monster. So, he said, "I'll give you £500 for them." I later learned that I was supposed to accept £5000. I said, "Yeh. Alright. That'll do. Thanks a lot." He said, "I can't pay you right away. I'll pay you in instalments as much as I can." At least he was honest enough not to just rip them off me. He sent me something like £145 and a couple of weeks later I went down to Brighton. Here's my band playing in the Aquarium[126] and I couldn't even bloody go in and see them. There were so many mods around. The whole of the south coast was turning on to mods. I'd done publicity, I'd got them into every single magazine you can possibly imagine. I'd made The High Numbers the hippest number in town.

Do you keep the cuttings?

Yeh, I kept them. But I threw them away after a while.

Was The Scene club still operating at this time?

Well, Kit pulled them out of The Scene club at put them on at the Marquee. The Scene club was still going because I put Jimmy James and The Vagabonds on there.

When did The Scene club close?

It closed down around 1966.

When did the mod thing start to fade, in your opinion?

About 1967, when acid came in.

Did it morph into hippie-ism or did it just die?

I had Captain Beefheart then. I had Jimmy James and The Vagabonds from 1965.

That's music. What about clothes?

I was into Continental clothes. Curtis Mayfield clothes.

What was the ultimate mod outfit from head to foot?

Tonik jacket, blue jeans, or Tonik trousers in a different colour.

126 The Who played The Florida Rooms in Brighton on Saturday August 2nd 1964. This was billed as an 'All Nite Rave'. The Florida Rooms were part of the Aquarium complex.

What is Tonik?

Tonik is a very metallic, heavy-fired cloth, cross-weave, which shines in the sun in green and red or blue and green. You can even get bronze and green or bronze and blue.

So that's the jacket and trousers?

A jacket with a seven or eight-inch centre vent. It's a stiffish quality cloth and it's tight. You wear tight sleeves, tight shoulders and a comfortable jacket with a centre vent. It was straight enough to be drape but small enough to be tight and you just did the top button up. You'd have a pair of Tonik trousers of a different colour, probably bronze and blue.

What shape?

Straight down but wide-ish. A bit like these trousers here. Hipsters with your belly button showing with a French jersey with a crew neck on it. Then you'd have a mod scarf, which is a scarf with a single twist in it so it flies out at the sides, and a pair of desert boots, and you're set for the weekend. If you wanna go on a scooter you got yourself a pair of dark glasses, maybe a stingy brim hat with an inch-wide brim, then an anorak and you'd sit on your scooter. You'd have your scooter and you'd have everything. You'd have your sleeping bag, your anorak, your parka[127].

What about the haircut?

French crew, razor barbered.

Did you use (hair) lacquer?

No. It was never lacquered. It was blow-dried. French crew was short at the front, a bit longer at the back. It was copied from the college boy cut. We were mostly blonde, fair geezers. I don't know why. We didn't have too many whiskers, like that Samuel Palmer picture. He hasn't got too many whiskers.[128]

127 The 'fishtail parka,' so called because the back was longer than the front, was developed in 1951 by the US military to give its troops weather protection during the Korean War. During the Sixties they could be purchased very cheaply at army surplus stores in Britain and became the identifying outer costume of the scooter mods. They came to public attention during the mod versus rocker fights in 1964. Mods would customise their parkas by adding fur to the hoods, dyeing them or stencilling letters and images on to the backs.
128 When I first visited Meaden in hospital he had cut a portrait of the Nineteenth century landscape painter Samuel Palmer out of a colour supplement and had taped it to his wall. He said he thought Palmer's haircut was very mod.

I believe that some mods were into make up?

Not really. They could have done but that's because effeminacy got into it.

Did you never hear of mods using make up?

Yeh, I heard about it, man, but I mean when you're out for four days on the trot man you don't listen to anything about make up. You really don't man. The practicalities of life are the basis of life. All you're trying to do is have a good time and try to keep yourself clean.

Were there ways of walking?

Yeh. You walked speed-wise which is you put both hands in your mod jacket, in your Tonik jacket, which had three-inch lapels and a seven-inch centre vent, and breast pleats to give it enough tuck. It was a very solid cloth, a very heavy cloth, so you'd tuck your hands in there and you'd have flaps on the pockets. You'd have your jeans turned up and you'd have Hush Puppies with a pair of white socks. You'd be walking with three other friends up Great Windmill Street or Wardour Street at five or six in the morning just as light is coming up. Your head is bent against the wind, you've got your head down, talking left to right and speaking left to right as well.

Was there a way of smoking?

Yeh, you smoked it as cool as you like, and you'd smoke king-size.

Inside your hands?

No! It's never covert. You drink black coffee, French coffee, cup of French, you know? You'd been on French blues. You smoke as cool as you can be, and you drink black coffee just to kick your system down, to keep your belly down because you'd been up for three nights already and your stomach is starting to rise.

Did mods read?

They'd read things of knowledgeable interest, like William Burroughs, if they ever got into William Burroughs, to find out what new drug trips were all about. They were interested in information on drugs, practical things.

I remember mods being interested in medical encyclopaedias.

That's it?

They would find them in bookshops and tear the relevant pages out. Sometimes they would steal drugs and wouldn't know their effects, so they'd have to look them up.

Well, you don't steal cos you're gonna get busted. You can't go trying to get busted. Your so gonna get busted by the clothes you're wearing and the scarf you've got around your neck, your little cardigan which is just down far enough that your belly button is showing. You've got your maroon Tonik trousers or your blue Levi jeans and your mod jacket, a pair of desert boots or a pair of boots or plimsolls, and it's enough to show that you're a bottom end man. Do you know what a bottom-end man means? It means a man has got enough bass end going on that he's actually walking around on the streets at four or five in the morning rather than sitting in some groovy pad in Notting Hill Gate

What did you do during weekday evenings?

Scene Club.

During the week?

Yeh. During the week. I had to go back home to go to work[129].

This was happening every night?

Yeh.

So, you were working five days a week and you were out every night?

It was always packed every night, with the real cliquey ones, the ones who really knew where it was at. They were dancing 'um um um um' to 'The Monkey Time'.

Were they taking pills during the week?

Just a couple to get you going.

How much was it costing you?

Well it cost two bob a pill in those days. You could get them on the National Health as well in those days.

Through your mother?

No. I used to get them for this anxiety thing. I'd say I'd been feeling anxious, "Do you think you could help me out on this one?" She'd say, "Well you'd better have some Drinamyl then. She'd give me

129 The Scene club was open every night of the week but Sunday.

thirty Drinamyl. I went back and took one of those little buggers and all my anxiety blocks disappeared, dissolved, and I was a free man. (At his point he asks me to switch off the recorder and then comes back with a statement.) Loyalty is the only thing that binds us together in the ghetto burgh of time and space. Modism is an aphorism for transcending the time and space. That's all.

What was the mod revolution all about?

My mod revolution was an undefined revolution against commodities and people, such as people were commodities. My parents treated me as a commodity.

Did they?

Yeh. Modism to me was a release, a sweet relief, from the burdens of mundane existence and at the end I had something like 250,000 mods running around the south coast, the south of England.

Did you go to the mod v rocker fights?

Yeh. I went to a few of the big fights. I saw them.

What were they like?

Too many of us and none of them. We overpowered them. It was like zap gunning them from a long distance.

What were the years of the fights?

They were '64, '65, '66 and '67. Then acid came in.[130]

How did it feel being involved?

That there was no focus, that The Who were letting us down. They should have been there with us. They should have been there. THEY SHOULD *HAVE BEEN THERE WITH US!!*

Did you feel elated?

I was elated when I was there. There were 15,000 kids on the street with you wearing exactly the same clothes. I was with Bob Bedford who is now a millionaire insurance broker. He was a mod, same as me, and he used to work on a music paper. We went down to

Opposite: Mods and Rockers fighting on Margate beach at Easter 1964. "There were too many of us," said Peter, "and none of them."

130 The first fights between mods and rockers took place at Clacton during the Easter weekend of 1964. This drew national attention to modism for the first time and prepared the way for the even bigger battles of Whitsun weekend, August 1964 when mods and rockers flooded to the seaside resorts of Clacton, Brighton, Margate, Southend and Bournemouth.

Hastings in 1967[131]. I knew it was over. It was falling apart. I went down because I wanted to see what the riots were all about. I had my own mod band, which was the Vagabonds. There should have been a conscious effort on then part of The Who to stick with the mods, not to go into pop art or those things, because pop art[132] was not where it was at.

Did mods follow pop art?

No, they did not. They never did. You can never say that about the mods. That was a sell out on The Who's part. I'm not being bitter now, but it was my revolution. I had 250,000 people on my side in uniform fighting for something which was un-clearly defined to me but, er...

Was 'My Generation' a mod song?[133]

Of course it was. There was a bit of a pride factor on Pete Townshend's part. I don't think he was too much into Jagger or anything like that, but he was talking more on pop songs and pop stars like Dylan and Lennon and Jagger.

He was becoming influenced by them?

Yeh, of course he was getting turned on to them. They were his friends. They were my friends as well. Jagger was my friend and I was Dylan's first publicist.

When did The Who lose their grip on the mod market?

I would say 1967, easy, maybe before that. I had the purism in Jimmy James and The Vagabonds

Yet while The Who were experimenting with pop art they were still wearing mod clothes.

I want to say now that I'm not letting down The Who. I'm just drawing a perspective on what the situation was. The situation was that here was a huge group of people, call it a market, I tend to call

131 Earlier he had dated his Hastings visit to 1966. Bob Bedford was a school friend of Norman Jopling's and wrote for *Record Mirror*.
132 The British Pop Art movement arose in the mid-Fifties. It appropriated images from commercial, sources such as advertising, comic books and mundane cultural objects and reinterpreted them as fine art. Pete Townshend became familiar with Pop Art while studying at Ealing Art College. The Who used similar techniques with their clothes, using medals (John Entwistle) the Union Jack flag (Pete Townshend) and motorway signs (Keith Moon). The cover of *The Who Sell Out* (1967) and *Who* (2019) were also tributes to Pop Art.
133 'My Generation' was released on October 29 1965. It reached number 2 in the UK pop charts.

them markets, but I try to be humane about it or human about it inasmuch as the mods were for me the revolutionary group. They were like the Viet Cong out in Cambodia, you know? There is the North Vietnamese army who are stolid troops and then there are the Viet Cong and they were like the mods. They've been fighting all the time. They've never let down the side. They have come in in strength. They've always been fighting as a minority group against the vast armour of the American army.

What did you think of the Quadrophenia *album?*[134]

Quadrophenia? Brilliant. I identified with it entirely. Talk about magic! There have been so many magic things that have happened in my life. Jimmy (the central character in the *Quadrophenia* story) could easily be Jimmy of Jimmy James and The Vagabonds. There's also the James Gang that Pete played with during the early Who tours. Jimmy is a mod – well, I am the mod who made mods out of The Who or made The Who into mods.

When did you feel they had let you down by no longer representing mods?

When I never got my ticket to the Brighton Pavilion – not the Brighton Pavilion, the Brighton Aquarium – that night. When I saw 50,000 kids queuing down there. There used to be queues outside The Scene club as well, but I never got my tickets that night.

It was mods who went to see The Who at the Marquee wasn't it?

Yeh. Well, they were people who dressed up in clothes.

Mod clothes?

Yeh.

What is the distinction between a mod and someone who wears mod clothes?

Mods stay up from Friday night through to Sunday morning. That's the difference. The rest dress up like they do [today] at David Bowie concerts.

They're just acting the part?

Yeh. But there were still 250,000 of us and that's more than any

---

134 *Quadrophenia* (1973) was a concept album that told the story of a troubled mod. Lyrics from Meaden's 'Zoot Suit' song were incorporated into the track 'Cut my Hair'. It was made into a film directed by Frank Roddam in 1979.

other cult group has ever got together.

Was modism based on style more than content?

Yeh, style. If you can dismiss life as having no substance, there was no substance. But if you can put life together as having substance, having a rationale, a reason to believe, then you have modism. It was via a pill, a few drinks, music to listen to and a style of your own that was so succinctly beautiful and self-contained. It was where privacy was everything and no one ever disturbed your privacy because you were all the same.

Doesn't it take a solid, well-organised society to support that sort of thing?

You have to stretch society. That's why they had policemen walking around.

Surely everyone couldn't live the mod life?

Anybody can be a mod. That's the beauty of it. Anyone can join the Vietcong, a freedom fighter.

Can you imagine 20-30 million British people staying out every weekend?

Yeh! That's what my dream is. That's what my dream was then.

Who would do the work?

They did. They work in the daytime.

Nurses can't be mods can they?

Of course they can. They were the best mods of all.

What if they're on night shift?

They'll come out in the daytime and go shopping with you. They'll have short haircuts and nurses are about the best mods of all because they're actual, practical people. Can't you understand? That's what mods are all about.

When did you stop being a mod?

I stopped after acid. I used to call myself a Black Tripper.

You became a hippie?

No, no. Hippies wore flowers. I had the Alikans jacket, a £300 jacket.

When did this happen?

That was when I brought Captain Beefheart[135] to Britain. It started when I had my mental breakdown, my nervous breakdown.

Opposite: Peter Meaden identified with Jimmy, the protagonist of Quadrophenia. Director Franc Roddam used Peter as a sounding board during the writing and filming

135 Captain Beefheart, Don Van Vliet (1941-2010), came to Britain with his Magic Band in January 1968 to promote his album *Safe as Milk* but was refused entry as he didn't have a work permit.

THE WHO FILMS PRESENT

QUADROPHENIA

A FILM BY FRANC RODDAM

Did that come as a result of your hard living?

Yeh. I had done three and a half years on the road with Jimmy James and The Vagabonds and they didn't believe in me any more. I was feeling that the structures of modism were breaking down. It has to be tightly sustained. That's a very important thing. Modism has to be sustained. There had to be a rigorous, rigid structure for modism to function.

What are the original mods doing today?

Owning garages, gambling clubs, bingo halls – making a lot of money probably. Mickey Tenner sends companies like Rank Xerox bust for £20,000. He does things like Exciting Lighting. He used to go to *Ready Steady Go!* and married Sandy Sarjeant (sic), the top mod dancer chick.

Was Ready Steady Go! *a mod programme?*

Not really. I used to have all my groups on there and they used to give me a hard time getting in, but I used to drink in the green room all the time.

Did you think of Cathy McGowan as a mod?

No. I was a mod. I was the only mod there. Michael Aldred was the compere. He co-compered with Cathy McGowan[136]. Vicki Wickham[137], who now manages Labelle[138], was a producer. But it wasn't mod. It pretended to be mod. It was a great programme, a fabulous programme, almost as good as *Cool for Cats*, Kent Walton's thing back in the early Sixties[139]. Cathy McGowan was great but modism was a pioneering venture and you have to take people along on this ride because there's not enough of you to sustain the strength that it needs to sustain it so you have to take everybody with you. Just as you had Phil the Greek standing there in front of the camera with his sawn-off double-barrelled

136 Michael Aldred (1945 - 1995) was a co-presenter on some of the early shows but Keith Fordyce (1928 - 2011) and Cathy McGowan became the main presenters.
137 Vicki Wickham (1939 -   ) went on to manage Dusty Springfield and Labelle. She co-wrote (with Simon Napier-Bell) Springfield's hit song 'You Don't Have To say You Love Me' and also (with Penny Valentine) her 2000 biography *Dancing With Demons*.
138 Labelle was a trio with Patti LaBelle, Nona Hendryx, and Sarah Dash.
139 Kent Walton (1917-2003) presented *Cool for Cats*, which was also made by Associated Rediffusion, between 1956-1961. It was one of the earliest British pop programmes to feature a live audience and each edition lasted 15 minutes.

shotgun saying; "These are my boys." He just opened his coat and pulled out this shotgun. That's where it's at, man. That's outrageousness. It's beyond outrageousness. It's all very well to do the things that Andrew (Oldham) did and some of the things that the Stones did but The Who, I mean – they blow up all sorts of things.

Is there anything else you'd like to say about The Who?

The Who are now coming back to the fact that we need responsibility in levity, which is to say that it has to be pure, it has to be fine, and when it's fine, it's right on.

Did The Who eventually become mods in your view?

I think Pete is the greatest mod of all time. And myself.

What about Roger?

Roger is Roger. He's the man who assaulted people with a meat axe.

Were you interested in them being mods or just in having them appeal to the mod market?

No. I made them into mods. They weren't mods. They've always said that they were never mods. It was just that they were my best mates and if I can't make my mates into the best mates you can ever make, which are mates you can be proud of, then I can't do anything for my friends. I've still kept in touch with them. All I can say is, as I said to Pete Townshend on the phone, "I only made you into The Who because I wanted you to be my mates."

POSTSCRIPT

I believe that the interview with Peter Meaden that forms the core of this book is a significant cultural document. It gives an unprecedented look into the mind of a man who was the most influential mod in the early-to-mid-Sixties and who managed for the first time to forge a link between an important British youth subculture and what was to become a major rock and roll band. The mod movement helped to establish The Who, not least by giving Pete Townshend the raw material for some of his greatest singles and one of his most celebrated albums, and The Who in turn helped to spread news of the mod movement by bringing it out of the all-nighter cellar clubs and on to the front pages of national newspapers.

Britain has excelled at producing youth subcultures from Fifties Teddy boys and rockers to Seventies punks and Seventies new romantics but no home-grown movement has had such a widespread and lasting impact on music, fashion, hair, television and lifestyle as mod. Although relatively short-lived in its initial thrust (there have been several revivals since) the approach to life it introduced has affected every subsequent subcultural uprising. The fact that we now expect teenagers wearing distinctly different clothes to have their own music, clubs, drugs and language dates back to mods. Teddy boys, for example, came about two or three years before rock and roll and started by liking the music of post-war dance bands like the one fronted by Ted Heath. Rockers liked Elvis, Jerry Lee Lewis and Chuck Berry but these American artists didn't write songs about British bikers or attempt to understand them.

Many of Britain's great rock and roll ambassadors however were deeply affected by mod; people like Rod Stewart, David Bowie, the Stones, The Small Faces, The Animals, Georgie Fame, Julie Driscoll, Zoot Money, Stevie Winwood, The Kinks, Marc

220

Bolan, Jeff Beck, Robert Plant, Andy Summers of The Police, The Who, Bryan Ferry and Eric Clapton. Mod introduced them to a very British form of dandyism, as well as to a culture where dancing, drugs, music, clothes and attitude were inextricably linked. Vitally, it introduced them to a seam of black American music that would remain a lifelong inspiration. It taught them that the most vigorous and compelling music was often to be found in the most obscure places – the B-sides of hard to find singles, LPs only available as expensive and rare imports, unadvertised after-hours clubs, West Indian shebeens, the bad side of town, the wrong side of the tracks.

Rod 'the mod' Stewart was an early worshiper of Sam Cooke and the hairstyle he's still wearing in his seventies is mod from root to tip. Marc Bolan considered himself a 'stylist' even before the word mod came into ordinary usage. The debonair Georgie Fame was a conduit between black American GIs based in the UK who had access to the latest US record releases and the weekend mods that frequented Soho.

When David Bowie was asked (in 1987) about the foundation of his fastidious interest in style and image he said; "I was into The Who. I was very much a mod in the Sixties. It was all (about) the hair, the right Fred Perry shirts, the length of the trousers being just so. It was all very French. The whole mod look, in England, came out of French fashions (which, at the time, were really good for guys) and Italian fashions. I liked the mod look. I was much more into it than Beatle jackets and stuff."

Many image icons not necessarily committed to the 48-hour weekend party lifestyle of the hardcore army still adopted the mod look. In this sense Twiggy and Sandy Shaw were mod. Samantha Juste from *Top of the Pops* and Cathy McGowan from *Ready Steady Go!* were mod. Even Michael Caine and Terence Stamp were a bit mod. David McCallum was modish in *The Man from U. N. C. L. E.* as was Diana Rigg in *The Avengers*. Many young fledgling creators who would make their impacts in the Seventies were introduced to style and image through the phenomenon of mod – fashion designer Paul Smith in Nottingham, impresario and club owner Peter Stringfellow in Sheffield, graphic designer Barney Bubbles in Twickenham, magazine editor Nick Logan in Leyton, broadcaster Janet Street Porter in Perivale, DJ Jeff Dexter in Camberwell.

Mod also affected later generations of British musicians such as Paul Weller (as a solo artist as well as with The Jam and Style Council), Dexy's Midnight Runners, Sleaford Mods, Arctic Monkeys, The Specials, Madness, Duffy and even Adele. Mark Ronson is a mod musician and producer. *The Face* (founded and edited by Nick Logan) was a mod magazine. *The Word, The Tube, Switch,* and *TGI Friday* were all mod TV programmes created in the likeness of *Ready Steady Go!* The clubs of Ibiza with their all-night electrobeats, dancing and ecstasy pills are mod clubs. Much contemporary window dressing, fashion photography and magazine layouts are built on mod innovations.

If you were a mod in the Sixties the way you looked and walked and held a cigarette were so important that, as Meaden said of one tailor, you'd "shoot the man if his shoulder pads [were] wrong." Teds might have cared about right jackets and the width of trouser legs, but the mods cared about the length of the vents in the jacket, the quality of the material and the source of the design. They were obsessed with detail. And the great thing about being a mod was that it traded in subtle forms of subversion. Everything about a Ted's uniform was obvious and calculated to offend and there weren't many jobs where you could wear the whole kit. A mod's outfit, by contrast, was smart. It outwitted the enemy by staying within the rules while tweaking them every which way.

If you weren't in the know you wouldn't have been able to put your finger on what was different about the style. The differences were small yet tremendously significant for the wearers. The hair would be shorter, modelled perhaps on what

Opposite: DJ Jeff Dexter, seen here in 1964 demonstrating The Twist, was an early London mod who frequented lunch time sessions at the Lyceum in Covent Garden where a strict dress code provoked subtle deviations

they'd seen actors wear in nouvelle vague French films, but it would be evenly cut and the sides would be a little longer than expected. There might also be some hair brushed back from the middle of the side or centre parting. It wasn't a huge gesture, but it was enough to signal to fellow mods an allegiance to modism.

It was the same with clothes. Nothing garish, outlandish or openly provocative was worn. It was all down to the cut of the trousers (straight-legged and not quite touching the shoes so that the bottoms flared out at the back), the way the jacket was buttoned, the width of the lapels, the material chosen for the suit. Mods could blend into any situation yet remain instantly recognisable to each other. They played the game but with daring, cheek and finesse.

Pete Townshend explained the phenomenon to an American readership in 1968. "As individuals these people were nothing. They were England's lowest common denominators. Not only were they young; they were lower class young. They had to submit to the middle class's way of dressing, speaking and acting to get the jobs that kept them alive. They had to do everything within terms of what existed around them. That made their way of getting something across that much more latently effective – the fact that they were hip and yet still, as far as granddad was concerned, exactly the same.

"It made the whole gesture so much more vital. It was incredible. As a force it was unbelievable. That was the bulge. That was England's bulge – all the war babies... Thousands and thousands of kids, too many kids, not enough teachers, not enough parents, not enough pills to go around. Everybody just grooving on being a mod."

For Peter Meaden mod was a religion substitute. It was something that saved him from the grey terrors of ordinariness he felt surrounded by in Edmonton, North London. It enabled him to feel free and gave purpose to his life. When dancing

Opposite: In 1968 Pete Townshend explained to an American readership that mods managed to incorporate hipness into clothing that appeared ostensibly conservative to an older generation

to the latest sounds from America he felt as though he momentarily transcended the ugliness of the world. He felt part of a community defined by its rituals. In fact, he loved it so much that he wanted to find a pop group that would act as ambassadors for this good life he had stumbled upon. That's when he came across The Who.

I must have first heard of the mods when they went in force to Margate and Brighton in 1964 and became embroiled in running fights with the leather-jacketed rockers. Although coming from similar working-class origins the rockers were the aesthetic opposites of the mods. Films starring Marlon Brando, Tony Curtis and James Dean inspired them rather than those directed by Truffaut and Chabrol. They loved Gene Vincent and Eddie Cochran rather than Curtis Mayfield, Smokey Robinson and Marvin Gaye. Their natural home was the Milk Bar or long-distance lorry driver's café rather than the all-night club, cellar bar or coffee house. They got their uplift from beer rather than amphetamines.

Teds had been involved in gang violence since the early Fifties and beatniks caused a riot at the 1960 Beaulieu Jazz Festival during a set by Acker Bilk, but there had never been a juvenile conflict on such a large scale or with such clearly defined ranks as the battles between mods and rockers. The front pages of all the newspapers were taken up with dramatic headlines and photographs of hurled deckchairs and swarming columns of teenagers while ordinary holidaymakers either retreated in fear or just looked bemused at the tribal conflict taking place in their midst. The children of the generation who'd fought the Nazi army on the beaches of France were now attacking each other on the beaches of Sussex, Essex and Kent.

Part of me was appalled and part was intrigued by these events. The Beatles had landed in New York for the first time only a few months before and their welcome by thousands of screaming girls seemed to vindicate my generation's tastes in music. The international popular vote proved our parents wrong. After years of being scoffed at for the music we loved and being told that it was just a 'craze' or a 'passing phase' the adult world was being forced to take notice.

The battles between the mods and rockers gave me the same sense. I felt that at last we had forced our way into the headlines despite the fact that teenagers, like children, were supposed to be seen but not heard. I didn't hate anyone or have the desire to cause anyone injury, but I could fully understand the attraction of being where the action was and the desire to dress to impress. The culture of English seaside resorts with their guesthouses, donkey rides, end of the pier entertainment, 'kiss me' hats and dads paddling with trouser legs rolled up was too restrained, unadventurous and dull. It seemed "awful cold" in words that Pete Townshend would later coin. It needed a bit of a shake up.

Grown ups saw it all as evidence of the malaise of the baby boomer generation. Some speculated that the trouble started with boys whose fathers had been away serving in the Second World War during their formative years, thus depriving them of masculine role models. Others thought the fights were substitutes for military action for the first wave of British young people since 1939 not to have to serve their country by doing National Service. The rockers, after all, dressed in jackets partly inspired by the leather jackets worn by USAF airmen during the war, and some mods wore khaki parka coats developed by the US military during the Korean conflict. Most adults agreed that a couple of years in the armed forces would tame these youngsters by instilling them with the values of discipline, hard work and respect for authority. (National Service had ended on the last day of 1960 and the last soldiers recruited under this scheme left the army in May 1963).

In 1964 I was caught between wanting to be considered a mod and hoping to be mistaken for a rocker. I was too young and easily persuaded to be seriously committed to either. Ever since I'd first heard rock and roll music it was associated with the styles favoured by rockers – greased-back hair, tight jeans, pointed shoes. The Beatles were the first popular group to challenge this uniform by wearing gusset-sided boots, knitted ties and hair free of pomade but even they had roots in the rocker world. They had dressed in leather and cowboy boots in their pre-Epstein and EMI days. But during their time in Hamburg they had also been influenced by the same continental fashions that would shape modism. Paul and John were in Paris in the autumn of 1960 when they first adopted the 'Beatle haircuts' that emulated the 'exis' (existentialists) of Hamburg. (Ringo was asked whether he was a mod or a rocker in *A Hard Day's Night* and quipped that he was a 'mocker.')

I could never be a real rocker because I only rode a butcher's bike and my 'leather' jacket was really made out of plastic, but I was reluctant to give up my commitment to tapered trousers and frustrated attempts at making my straight hair curl. But by 1965 I had made the transition. I had voted mod. It was only many years later that I realised just how much of a latecomer I had been. For metropolitans like Peter Meaden the movement was already well in decline by 1965 and, anyway, I never went the whole pill-popping hog. I liked the style, the music and the feeling of being associated with a national youth movement that wasn't controlled or directed by adults, but I wasn't willing to break the law or experiment on my brain to gain full membership.

I can't recall the exact moment of conversion, but it would have been signalled by the last application of Brylcreem in 1965, a step at the time that would have been as dramatic as an AA member's smashing of whisky bottles. I was avidly reading *Rave*, a magazine that made its debut in February 1964, and combined reportage on pop with information on fashion ("a frank look at today's pop world" as it said on the cover). *Rave* kept you up to

Opposite: Rave magazine, launched in February 1964, broadcast London's mod trends to the whole country. Dennis (no surname given) had a monthly column announcing the latest male fashion accessories

JUST DENNIS

Got a great new outfit this month — really knockout! And while I was travelling about getting it I couldn't help but notice the fabulous choice of shoes there is now. I've shown just a selection at the bottom.

My check shirt in black and white, came from Cue, the Austin Reed boutique in Regent Street. Button-down super high collar in American style. Price 59s. 6d.

The belt I bought from Lord John in Carnaby Street. It's white leather with a metal buckle. Terrific! Price 19s. 11d.

These black, slightly shiny hipster-style trousers, come from The Trouser Shop at Adam W.1. in Kingly Street. Front pockets but no back ones. Slightly flared trousers and, of course, wide belt loops. Price £3 19s. 6d.

I rate these black and white shoes the greatest. They're called Climax, and have a driving heel. Price £4 19s. 6d. From Ravel in Carnaby Street.

I don't know what your taste in shoes is. But I had a lot of fun having a look at this lot:-

A. "Pacemaker" by Ravel. £4 19s. 6d.
B. Merrywell. 59s. 11d.
C. Merrywell. 59s. 11d.
D. Dolcis. 69s. 11d.
E. From Saxone and Lilley & Skinner. 59s. 11d.
F. Saxone and Lilley & Skinner. 79s. 11d.
G. From Ravel. £4 19s. 6d.
H. From Lennards. 59s. 11d.
I. Called "Vivian". From Ravel £6 19s. 6d.
J. From Merrywell. 59s. 11d.
K. From Saxone and Lilley & Skinner. 59s. 11d.
L. Called "Brummel". From Ravel. £5 19s. 6d.
M. From Saxone and Lilley & Skinner. 59s. 11d.

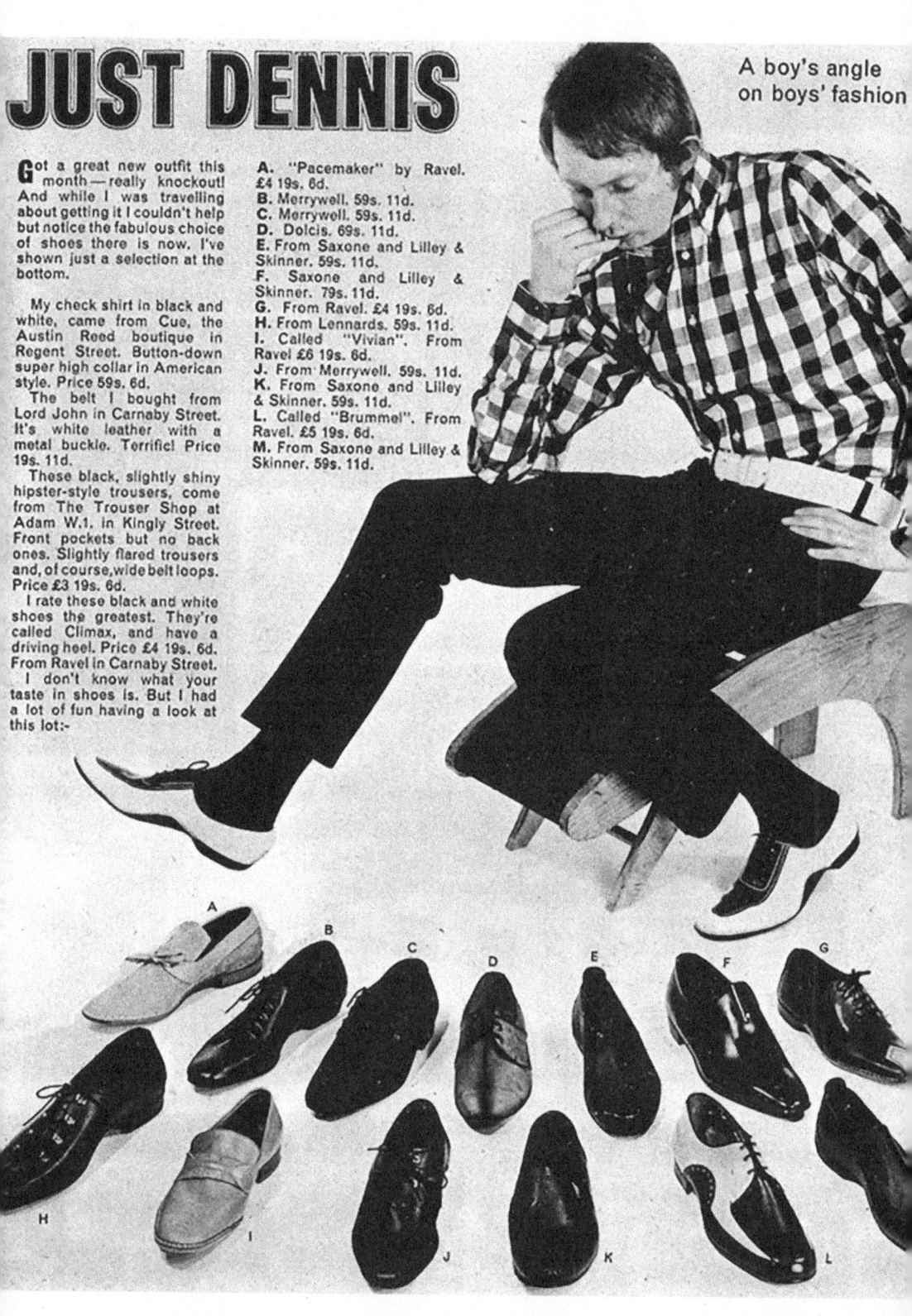

date with what was happening in London, what was 'in' or 'out' and allowed girls to read what boys were thinking and boys to read what girls were thinking. To use a later term, it was a 'unisex' magazine. This is where I read an interview with Roger Daltrey where he talked of drugs (something I had never heard a pop star discuss before), claiming that they weren't dangerous. I was also impressed with the look of The Small Faces – the Carnaby Street jackets, hipster trousers, wide leather belts and lace up shoes.

Someone referred to only as Dennis wrote a monthly column for *Rave* (Just Dennis) pointing out what was IN or OUT and predicting what might be IN by the end of the year. He apparently worked for the magazine's art department and his tips were those of a sophisticated young Londoner with media, fashion and music connections working in the heart of the fastest moving city in Britain. Rave was based in Tower House, Southampton Street, (Covent Garden), a short walk away both from where *Ready Steady Go!* was recorded and the fashion boutiques of Carnaby Street and Kingley Street.

At the end of 1965 I made my first visit to Carnaby Street and bought a pair of Levi jeans for 59 shillings and 11 pence (an old penny short of three pounds). In those days Carnaby Street had traffic and ordinary shops (the pipe and tobacco shop Inderwick's was at number 45) mixed in with the boutiques. In Northampton, one of the closest big towns to where I lived, I bought a striped Madras jacket for around five pounds. I later bought a pair of white slip-on shoes with 'driving heels' from Ravel in Carnaby Street. Putting this combination together with white socks and a white roll-neck made me feel distinctively mod. (The most advanced London mods had already abandoned Madras jackets. *The Sunday Times Magazine* reported in August 1964 "American styles are out, like Madras cotton jackets ..." quoting a 17-year old mod from Streatham as saying "It's suits now, and basket shoes.")

I liked the fact that mods always seemed to be two steps ahead of everyone else in their fashion choices and musical tastes. They moved with the swiftness of professional trend spotters but once they succeeded in influencing a sizeable number of early-adopters they were forced to abandon the good new thing or risk their position as market leaders. A spirit of restlessness was integral to their approach to life. They were forever on the move. As *Melody Maker* wryly commented at the time when covering the phenomenon: "The trouble with writing about mods is they've probably changed by the time you've finished typing." Reflecting on the fact that he had access to a pre-release white label of the Velvet Underground's debut album in 1966, David Bowie commented; "Not only was I able to cover a Velvet's song before anyone else in the world, I actually did it before the album came out. Now that's the essence of Mod."

By 1966 I had started paying visits to Northampton's only male boutique where one of the town's coolest mods worked. (Before boutiques there were only 'gentlemen's outfitters' for teenage boys – no music, no enticing displays and few choices of cut or style.) Danny Smedley, the shop's main assistant, had already gone one step beyond the normal mod haircut by growing his hair very long at the back and in front of the ears then hacking the bit that was normally backcombed until it stuck up in ragged spikes. It made him look dissolute and slightly unkempt. It was a Rod Stewart haircut before Rod Stewart, caught midway between French crews and hippy locks.

Danny had his hair razor-cut to give it the edgy look and then had the ends singed with a lighted wax taper to give it better texture. He got some of his fashion tips from *Town*, one of the great British men's magazines of the Seventies that offered a mixture of style, fiction, reviews and general features. In September 1962 it had been the first magazine to cover the mod phenomenon when it interviewed and photographed three young 'faces' one of whom was a young Marc Bolan (then Mark

Feld). I supplemented my reading of *Rave* with the more adult coverage of *Town* and this was where I was tipped off about Granny Takes A Trip, Hung on You and other new fashion outlets opening in Chelsea along the King's Road.

Two records that summed up mod for me at the time were Robert Parker's 'Let's Go Baby (Where the Action Is)' (1966) and Dobie Gray's 'The In Crowd' (1964). To be a mod was not only to be at the cutting edge of youth fashion but also to know all the hottest records, clubs, coffee bars, boutiques, trends and parties. Missing out on a weekend's activity was to run the risk of being completely out of touch and being out of touch was one of the worst sins a mod could commit. There were no feelings of nostalgia to be found in the mods that I knew. They lived entirely in the present moment with a keen eye on the future.

Both of these records, although written by Americans ('Let's Go Baby' by Parker himself, 'The In Crowd' by Billy Page), put their finger on the thrill of belonging to a pioneering group of contemporaries – a group that was distinguished by its classiness and and which set trends rather than followed them. As Page wrote in 'The In Crowd' – "If it's square, we ain't there." The jive language of the Fifties, and the outlook it represented, was still firmly in place. You were either fusty, unfashionable and conformist ('square'), or you were modern, up to date and progressive ('with it').

It was when I started working in the town of Rugby in 1966 that for the first time I got to hang out with real mods. The local crowd would be out drinking and perhaps catching a band at the Benn Hall on a Saturday night before driving off to all-nighters at celebrated clubs like The Twisted Wheel in Manchester, The Mojo in Sheffield or The Gaff in Banbury. On Sunday morning they would sit silently in the Il Cadore coffee bar with their pupils dilated as the effects of the amphetamines wore off. My best mate Andy, with whom I'd just recently been exploring Carnaby Street and the King's Road, had moved to Rugby and

Opposite: Robert Parker's 1966 single 'Let's Go Baby (Where the Action Is)' summed up the essence of mod for Steve Turner

232

had become accepted by this crowd. He had been living alone with his father after his parents divorced and was consequently not as supervised as the rest of us.

I envied Andy's advance from callow schoolboy to revered mod. By dint of wearing the right clothes and going to the right places he'd become a leader among this group of outcasts and misfits. He became noticeably cooler in his demeanour, saying a lot less but seemingly meaning a lot more with what he did say. His life became swathed in mystery and legend. He started taking drugs, then selling them and finally stealing them. I went to call for him one afternoon and discovered from his flat mate that he'd 'gone away.' I wondered when he'd be back. "No, he's gone away," his friend repeated, with a more serious intonation. "He's in a borstal." He'd been caught breaking into a pharmacy to steal amphetamines.

I felt left behind. Not only had Andy broken his ties with home and become a local mod legend but he was now doing time. I was a mere imitator. I was a substitute for another guy. I looked pretty mod, but my heels were high. When Andy was released from borstal he was tougher and more prone to take risks. He read William Burroughs' novels to become acquainted with the twilight world of junkies and tore pages out of medical encyclopedias he found in W. H. Smith & Son to better understand the likely effects of all the drugs that were coming his way.

By 1967 most mods (including Andy) had morphed into hippies. It wasn't in the nature of modism to stand still. It was constantly pressing forward in search of the next big thing. The hair got longer, the jeans wider, the coats longer and the music more reflective. It was not such a big step for those who'd been taking amphetamines and hash to take LSD and once that had happened everything changed. By suppressing anxiety and self-consciousness amphetamines gave greater freedom to the body. Hallucinogenics, by contrast, appeared to free the mind.

Hippies would become known for their thoughts and peaceful intentions rather than their great dances.

The Who followed the same path. One minute it was polo shirts, Union Jack blazers and three-minute singles about alienation and the next it was satin blouses, fringed jackets and concept albums about self-realisation. Pete Townshend didn't see this as the abandonment of his early mod-inspired vision of intense living but the fulfilment of a desire to break out, transcend and expand. He might as well have sung; "Hope I die and get reborn before I get old." On *Quadrophenia* he blended the restlessness and thrill-seeking that characterised mod with symbolism drawn from his more recent encounters with eastern mysticism.

I met Peter Meaden in May 1975, over a decade after the high point of the mod era. He was 33 years old. He still maintained a modish image even though he was no longer as sartorially sharp as he had been in his early twenties and a thickening waist limited his style choices. His wiry sandy-coloured hair was cut short, he wore straight-legged trousers and white shoes and had his shirts tailor-made. He chain-smoked throughout our conversation, still spoke of 'chicks' and 'spades' and had a habit of ending long speeches with the word 'man.'

I had been commissioned to write the text for a deluxe book of The Who's music (*A Decade of The Who*). The plan was to do a number of stories about different aspects of the band and scatter them throughout the songbook rather than having continuous text. I knew of Peter's significance in the group's early career and thought he'd make an excellent interview. I tracked him down through the publisher of 'I Am the Face' the song he'd written for The Who (as The High Numbers) for their debut single on the Fontana label. I was given a phone number. When I called up the person at the other end said, "I think he's on M1." I assumed I must be calling a motorway service station or even a road construction company but soon learned that I was calling a psychiatric hospital in Woodford Bridge, Essex. He was being held in Ward M1.

Peter was being treated for a breakdown. He didn't give me the full details, only that it had something to do with him having run riot in someone's flat in Belsize Park throwing pots of paint over the walls. It wasn't the first time he'd done this sort of thing and by the time he was 30 his mental instability was bad enough that he'd become difficult to employ. Whatever he'd achieved in the early-Sixties counted for nothing in the new decade.

I recently discovered a slip of paper that had been by my 'phone during this first call. Some of his comments sounded odd enough to me at the time to think it worthwhile writing them down; "I have been told to help you by higher things"; "It's a positive universe Pete" (I think at this point he was recounting what the higher things had told him); "You're not to worry about things. All these things make us stronger so that when we get to the grey place..."; "I'm the ultimate loser. I'm the ultimate winner though because I'm going into politics."

It was strange stuff, but he was friendly, keen to talk and quick to set up a date. For our first interview, on May 12, 1975, he was given a day release and came to my flat in London's West End where we spent an afternoon talking. For the second interview a few days later I went to the hospital where he had a private room with a single bed and a couple of chairs. On the wall he had taped a portrait of the Nineteenth century landscape painter Samuel Palmer that he had torn from a Sunday newspaper magazine. He'd put it there, he said, because he thought Palmer had a great mod haircut.

The interviews were some of the most interesting and revealing that I've ever done. They were interesting not only because he was authoritative on an area of popular culture that was very under-documented but also because he spoke in a way that imitated the experiences he was describing. He was talking about excitement, speed and living on the edge and he sounded excited, speedy and edgy. The medium was the message. He seemed to be so pleased to be asked to open up about this era that the words just flew out of him, the transcribed replies often going on for pages.

A psychiatric report made by the hospital during this time described his state of mind like this; "He was rather hypomanic at the time, being excitable in manner with pressure of speech and on discharge it was felt that he may either have had an anxiety state or a hypomanic episode." (Hypomania is a mood state characterized by persistent lack of inhibition and pervasive euphoria with or without irritable moods but less severe than full mania.)

Looking back over what he said from a vantage point of almost 50 years I'm still impressed at the vitality of his images. He would almost always come up with a pictorial equivalent of an emotion; mod solidarity was explained in terms of bullfighters, the 'groove' of a Friday night was likened to a match being rubbed against an abrasive surface and the camaraderie of The Who was compared to a painting of First World War artillery soldiers manning a machine gun.

Some of the phrases that he coined during our talks have gone on to become part of the mod revivalist lexicon – like his comparison of the mods to the Viet Cong and his definition of the mod life as "clean living under difficult circumstances." The 'clean living' quote has gone on to emblazon posters, parkas, iPad covers and tee shirts as well as to become the subtitle of both a book and an album. It was used on the back cover of the *Quadrophenia* movie soundtrack album. The cyclist Bradley Wiggins quoted it in his 2019 Sky TV documentary on mods and it has been registered as a trademark in the US. The *Daily Mirror* columnist and author Tony Parsons told me in the Seventies that he used the interview when building the character of the mod David Lazar in his novel *Limelight Blues* and some of Lazar's conversation was clearly borrowed from what Peter had said.

He may have been medicated when we spoke and one effect of this was that the sounds of particular words would lead his mind down unrelated paths linked only by loose association. He once explained it to me as "four-way puns which are very complicated, and what comes out of your mouth is perhaps only a fifth of what could come out." Speaking of emotional 'tangle ups' suggested the tango which in turn led to thoughts of dancing, and dancing reminded him of 'You Gotta Dance to Keep from Crying' by The Miracles, a song he referred to several times during the interviews.

This idea behind this song – that dancing (and implicitly, music) could provide a way of blocking out sorrow – was a recurring theme and opened up a dark side to his obsessions. If mod offered a form of salvation – and he actually said that mod was his religion – what was it saving him from? The answer was a life of loneliness, frustration and the mundane. At one point he told me that what he liked about the mod attitude was that it was so anti "family London"

I could see what he meant. There was no place in the mod life for menial things. Anything boring could immediately be cut out because you were ultimately responsible to no one. Everything in this new life was defined by what happened during the leisure hours. It was an escape from family ties, domestic routines and civic duties. Mods liked to live at home, not because they liked sharing and caring, but because they knew that their mothers would do all the boring things for them. Mothers provided eggs, bacon, clean sheets, soap and toothpaste. Pete Townshend again; "Substitute you for my mum/ At least I'll get my washing done."

Opposite: The theme of The Miracles' 1963 hit 'I Gotta Dance to Keep from Crying' became part of Peter Meaden's philosophy of mod

Peter found meaningful relationships hard to forge. He had close mates when the mod movement was in full swing but what kept them together were shared highs rather than compassion and intimacy. There was little sense of community beyond the dance floor and many of the mods, as I discovered

when writing this book, didn't even know each other's surnames or home districts. They never discussed feelings, backgrounds or parents. There may have been an unintended deeper significance to their use of the word 'faces' because that's where the mutual interest in each other began and ended. When he reflected on the era Peter Meaden recalled the highlight as dancing alone in a crowd and the greatest benefit of being at The Scene club was that no one invaded his private space.

He didn't have a high view of women. Although there were female mods, Peter was wary of them. He resisted attachment because he saw females as a threat to his independence, privacy, spontaneity and self-devotion. I never heard him speak warmly, tenderly or longingly about a woman. On the other hand, he didn't leer. His idea of a fulfilled sex life was self-pleasure and he saw no advantage in getting a woman involved, except perhaps in a massage parlour or a brothel. Masturbation, like mod, offered protection from getting caught up in family life.

Reading his thoughts now I can detect a commitment to purity and precision that had counterparts in Thirties Germany. He wasn't a racist or a fascist (I never heard him say anything racially offensive) but his obsession with style, survival and separation from the masses had some of the elements that in another country and another generation led to Nazi uniforms, eugenics and the creation of a master race rather than a subculture and dance music.

His brother Gerald recalls him going through a teenage phase of collecting Nazi memorabilia and late in his life he enthused to me about *Spear of Destiny* by Trevor Ravenscroft, a book that speculated that the Nazis searched for the spear thrust into the side of Christ on the cross, believing it to have magical powers. He was also a big fan of Norman Spinrad's alternative history novel *The Iron Dream* in which Hitler flees

240

Germany in 1919 to become an American pulp SciFi writer.

Although I'm unsure of the exact sequence of events I know my interviews happened around the same time as he discovered the Steve Gibbons Band and started looking after them under the auspices of The Who's manager Bill Curbishley. A decade after losing The Who to Kit Lambert and Chris Stamp he was mates again with Pete, John, Roger and Keith and working out of offices in Wardour Street, Soho, not far from his old stomping ground of Ham Yard and Great Windmill Street.

We stayed in touch after all my work was completed on *A Decade of The Who*. I liked Peter. He had none of the aggression or ruthlessness that often characterises music business entrepreneurs and his continued avoidance of adult responsibilities meant that he could afford to remain eternally boyish. He was open to new experiences and avoided passing judgement on anything until he'd experienced it for himself. I think he was a great believer in the value of the happy accident and knew that the next big thing was almost certainly to be found in an unlikely place.

I took him to see Larry Norman, a Christian singer from America with shoulder length blonde hair, who was performing an acoustic set to a sell-out audience at the Albert Hall. Norman was barely known outside of the religious market but that didn't bother Peter. He was up for it. He came away impressed both by Norman's stage presence and his ability to fill one of London's most prestigious venues without the aid of the mainstream media. He seemed to appreciate anyone with a defined image and a well targeted demographic. "What I couldn't understand was what market he was hitting on," he told me afterwards. "He's not a chart artist. Yet, the Albert Hall, for an American, is pretty heavy. Right?"

A receptionist at The Who's office, Caroline Guinness (now Caroline Guinness McGann), had a friend called Alan Jones

who worked at Malcolm McLaren and Vivienne Westwood's Chelsea clothing store Sex. Jones would enthuse to anyone who'd care to listen about a new unsigned band called the Sex Pistols that he was friendly with and DJ'd for. As a result, I went with Peter to see them at the 100 Club on Oxford Street in September 1976 and both of us came away feeling that something similar to what had happened with The Who and the mods was happening with the Pistols and their pogoing legions. Just as Peter had found a band to provide a focal point for mods, so manager McLaren was manipulating the Sex Pistols to represent the emerging punks.

Yet, much as he could appreciate what was happening in 1976, he never showed any interest in managing a young punk band. His focus was the Steve Gibbons Band from Birmingham. In the Seventies Gibbons had been with the Uglys and his current bass player, Trevor Burton, had played with The Move. The Steve Gibbons Band was not punk. Gibbons had long thick hair and a dark beard and idolised Elvis, Chuck Berry and Bob Dylan, the very people that punks claimed they wanted to forget.

Peter involved himself with the band with all the seriousness that he'd once applied to The Who and hustled his music journalist friends in the same way he had done a decade earlier. He sketched out band logos on scraps of paper and tried to encourage Burton to dress in leather and wear an iron cross around his neck. One of his early ideas was to rename them the Iron Boys. He got them work as a support act to The Who and later an American tour in their own right. In May 1977 I met up with Peter in LA where he was accompanying Gibbons as he performed at the Whisky A-Go-Go on Sunset Strip and we lunched in a restaurant close to the Chateau Marmont, the legendary hotel for touring rock bands.

Peter was typical of a breed of bright Grammar School boys whose appetite for music and style had distracted him from

Opposite:
The author
accompanied
Peter Meaden
to see the
Sex Pistols
at London's
100 Club in
1976. The
zeitgeisty air
of expectation
reminded Peter
of seeing The
Who for the
first time at
the Goldhawk
Social Club in
1964

academic study. Instead of using his intellect to explore maths or physics he used it to understand, and later work with, the minutiae of popular culture and in his way developed expertise in image, advertising, music, costume, media and behaviour. The managers, agents and PR people who shaped the music of the Fifties were often early school leavers who sold pop stars to teenagers in the same way that their type had once sold cheap suits or jewellery to customers in the East End. This was show business, not art. The Seventies intake was different. The influences for the new breed of manager and image-maker like Andrew Oldham, who masterminded the early stage of The Rolling Stones' career, were French films, Beat poetry, jazz, Madison Avenue, pop art and the blues.

Peter's problem as a manager, publicist and marketing strategist was that although he had a finely tuned instinct for music, style and youth subculture he had no matching business savvy. He wasn't ruthless enough to survive in the Tin Pan Alley jungle. He was disorganised and didn't care much about wealth or possessions. Some of the saddest comments he made to me were about how he handed over The Who to the far more effective and well financed Kit Lambert for a measly sum and how, above all, he'd only wanted The Who to be his mates. He was more upset about losing his friends than losing a fortune.

Opposite:
Peter at the
back of his
parents' house
in Edmonton.
This was where
he had early
dreams of
making it in the
music business
and where in
1965 he hosted
Chuck Berry

In the end his drug intake impaired his chances of ever repeating his success with The High Numbers with any other acts. Word got around that he wasn't reliable, and this irked him. It made him want to prove himself. The year 1978 should have been a good year for him. He'd recently learned that huge Who fan Nik Cohn, author of the *New York* magazine feature on Brooklyn disco life that had been used as the basis for the film *Saturday Night Fever*, had said that his real inspiration for the characters in his (largely fictionalised) story had come not from New York but from Shepherd's Bush circa 1964.

Cohn believed that youth subcultures had the same constituent elements regardless of the decade and location and therefore all he needed to do was to embellish his memory of the key mod faces to turn them into inhabitants of the emerging New York disco scene. Peter reasoned that by logical implication he was the model for the sharp dressing main character Tony Manero, played in the movie by John Travolta, who lived only for dancing, clothing, grooming and the weekend.

Working at Bill Curbishley's Trinifold company office in Wardour Street in 1978 put Peter into the orbit of the makers of the film of *Quadrophenia*, scheduled to shoot later that year in London and Brighton. His first-hand memories of mod life were of great interest to director Franc Roddam who would often drop by the office. Peter was already Manero, as played by Travolta; now he could also become Jimmy, as played by Phil Daniels; The Jimmy who, when told that everyone is the same underneath, would retort; "Look, I don't wanna be the same as everybody else. That's why I'm a mod, see? I mean, you gotta be somebody, ain't ya, or you might as well jump in the sea and drown."

The last time I saw Peter was in June of that year when he came to hear me give a poetry reading in a small theatre near Waterloo station. We went for a drink afterwards and his conversation seemed unusually bleak and incoherent. He was talking about the end of the world, and also religion; "Who's the one then?" he asked me, apropos of nothing. "Is it Meher Baba or Jesus?" He sometimes heard voices in his head that gave him instructions. He told me that the best book dealing with madness was Frances Farmer's *Will There Really Be A Morning* because she captured the essence of what it was to fear that you were losing your mind.

In July I joined Paul Simon on a short tour of Israel where he was supported by gospel singer Jessy Dixon. I wrote a feature about Dixon for *Melody Maker* and Peter suggested that I should write it under a new pseudonym. I think the original idea was that I could have many different journalistic lives if I invented other characters. I don't know the reason why this interview was the first, and only time I ever did it – maybe because I was a listed contributor to *NME* and wanted to avoid a conflict of interests – but it was published under the bi-line of Johnny someone-or-other, a name Peter invented for me.

On a day early in August I called Trinifold and was put through to Chris Chappel, at that time working as a tour manager with The Who. "Is Pete there? I asked him. "He's dead," said Chappel. He said it in such an abrupt way that I thought he was joking; that he was meaning "Pete's dead in the head" or "Pete's a dead loss." But he was serious. Peter had died on July 29 in his bedroom at his parents' home in North London, the same sort of terraced house featured in the picture insert of the *Quadrophenia* album. Less than six weeks later Keith Moon died, thereby ending the career of The Who in its original form.

I'd been at what would be the original band's final performance at Shepperton Studios on May 25 when Moon had thrown his sticks into the air for the last time, linked arms with Pete, John and Roger and bowed before the audience. Jeff Stein filmed this private show put on in front of a selected audience of hard-core fans for the documentary *The Kids Are Alright*. All of us in the invited audience were taken outside and had to form four equal lines behind Pete, John, Roger and Keith while Terry O'Neill, positioned in a cradle suspended from a crane, photographed us for a potential cover.

I went to Peter's funeral in Southgate, North London. Bill Curbishley was there with his wife Jackie but none of the band, who I think were in America. I didn't see anyone from his time as a mod and very few from his career in the music business. Before the service a handful of us met at his parents'

IN
EVER LOVING MEMORY
OF
PETER ALEXANDER EDWIN
MEADEN
DIED JULY 29th 1978
AGED 36 YEARS

home at 7 Cuthbert Road, the house where he'd dreamed of advertising slogans, played with names for The Who and then killed himself with barbiturates and vodka. His parents were elderly and, I felt, slightly bemused by what had happened.

The home, comfortable as it was, was everything that Peter had rebelled against. Its very ordinariness was what had propelled him into a world of excitement, danger and glamour. He had brought Chuck Berry here in January 1965 after the singer played at The Regal Theatre, Edmonton. As I sat in this house I kept thinking of what Peter had told me about the appeal of mod being the fact that it was "anti family London." The music business mourners seemed out of place among the armchairs, old furniture, china teacups and cucumber sandwiches.

I could understand what made Peter and many others like him reject the stability, delicateness and regularity of post-war domesticity. It was a feeling expressed so well by Pete Townshend in such Who songs as 'Anyway, Anyhow, Anywhere' and 'My Generation.' It was a feeling expressed by Jack Kerouac in *On the Road*, a book that had inspired Peter even before he became a mod. In the novel Sal Paradise (based on Kerouac) finds himself in "the colored section" of Denver, "wishing I were a Negro, feeling that the best the white world had offered was not enough ecstasy for me, not enough life, joy, kicks, darkness, music, not enough night."

That's what Peter was also searching for. His heroes in his mod days, like Kerouac's, were typically black – Curtis Mayfield, Smokey Robinson, Major Lance, Chuck Berry – and his goal in life was to find ecstasy, joy and kicks, much of it through music, most of it at night. It was a search that characterised the subculture of mod and the teens of the sixties. It continues to characterise youthful questing from hip-hop to club culture, which is why Peter Meaden is a man worth getting to know and why his words continue to sound contemporary.

Opposite: Peter Meaden's grave in Southgate Cemetery, North London. Stanley, was buried in the same plot in 1992

WHERE ARE THEY NOW?

Michael Aldred (1945 - 1995)

When he appeared on *Ready Steady Go!* at the age of 18 he was the youngest presenter on British TV. He went on to become a music journalist, songwriter, and record producer, moving to America in the Seventies. He died in London after contracting HIV Aids in 1995.

Elkan Allen (1922 - 2006)

As Head of Entertainment for Associated-Rediffusion, Allen produced such shows as *Take Your Pick* and *Double Your Money*. In 1963 he devised *Ready Steady Go!* Later in the Sixties he returned to print journalism and became TV Editor for *The Sunday Times*

Peter Anders (1941 - 2016)

Anders (born Andreoli) had a chequered career because of his addiction to hard drugs. He started singing with a doowop group, The Videls, in 1956, which eventually led to a writing deal for him and his creative partner Vini Poncia with Hill & Range. After meeting producer Phil Spector they wrote for his acts Darlene Love, The Crystals and the Ronettes. In 1965 Elvis recorded their song 'Harlem Holiday' for his movie *Harum Scarum*. Drugs interfered with his ability to work although he managed to record The Anders and Poncia Album in 1969. After coming to England to head up production at Tamla Motown he was dismissed by the company in 1972 and refused entry back into Britain in 1977 because of earlier drug offences. There followed years of obscurity during which he went to rehab seven times. He then worked outside the music business to avoid temptation. In 2010 he made a comeback album *So Far*. He died in 2016.

Philip Andronicos (1945 -   )

Known as 'Phil the Greek' because people couldn't pronounce his surname. Andronicos was a hairdresser and then a teacher at the Vidal Sassoon Academy in London. Among the mods he had a reputation for being both flashy and tough. He worked as a road manager for The Pretty Things for a short time. He says his 'real life' began when he married an Italian girl, moved to Italy, got a pilot's license, and eventually flew Boeing 747s for Al Italia. Following a divorce, he moved to America and brokered aircraft before starting his own charter airline, Air America Caribbean, in 2010. He lives in Florida.

Keith Altham (1941 -   )

Altham worked for *Fabulous* magazine from its beginning in January 1964 before becoming a feature writer for *New Musical Express* interviewing all the top acts of the era. In 1971 he formed K. A. Publicity which went on to represent acts such as The Stones, T. Rex, Slade, Rod Stewart, The Who, The Police and The Steve Gibbons Band.

Peter Asher (1944 -   )

After making a name for himself as half of the singing duo Peter and Gordon, scoring hits in both Britain and America, Asher headed Apple's A&R department. He later moved to Los Angeles where he managed and produced James Taylor and Linda Ronstadt. Since the early Noughties he has returned to performing, initially with Gordon Waller, and later with Jeremy Clyde and Albert Lee. He was awarded a CBE in 2015.

Don Black (1938 -   )

Brother to Cyril Blackstone, who married the future Scene DJ Sandra Young, Don Black is one of Britain's most prolific and successful lyricists. Among his best-known works are 'Born Free' (Matt Monro), 'Thunderball' (Tom Jones), 'Diamonds are Forever' (Shirley Bassey), 'Ben' (Michael Jackson), 'To Sir With Love' (Lulu), 'Take That Look Off Your Face' (Marti Webb), 'Love Changes Everything' (Michael Ball), and 'Surrender' (k. d. lang). His most successful writing partnerships have been with musicians John Barry, A. R. Rahman, and Andrew Lloyd Webber. He lives in London.

Cyril Blackstone (1935 -   )

Brother to lyricist Don Black, Cyril worked for a music publishing company in Soho and married Sandra Lane in 1960. Together they had a daughter, Karen. He remarried in 1964 and later went to America with Karen and his new wife Sylvia. He has never heard from Sandra since she left him and has no idea what happened to her. He and Sylvia live in the Miami area.

Sandra Blackstone (1939 -   )

Sandra Blackstone was born as Sandra Lane in Portsmouth. She came to London in the late Fifties and married Cyril Blackstone in 1960. A daughter, Karen, was born that year but the marriage broke up shortly after and Sandra walked out of the home leaving Blackstone with the child. In 1963 she began working as a DJ at The Scene and became renowned among the mods for her choice of rare American R&B tracks which she accessed from black GIs stationed in the UK. Adverts for the club announced that Tuesday and Wednesday nights were 'Off The Record with Sandra.' When the club closed in 1966, she disappeared without trace.

Lionel Blake (1937 - 2018)

Born and raised on a farm in South Africa, Blake came to Britain in 1958. He worked as an accountant for Mobil Oil before managing the clubs Lachelle, La Discotheque and The

Scene in London. He spent three years in Vietnam as a war photographer and later ran a floating restaurant in Singapore. In the Seventies he returned to London and accountancy, working for a company run by Ted Syms, brother of the actress Sylvia Syms. He lived in Bayswater, West London.

Tony Calder (1943 - 2018)

Calder began working with Andrew Oldham after starting out as a ballroom DJ and then a press officer for Decca. They went on the form Immediate Records which had great success with The Nice, P. P. Arnold, The Small Faces, Chris Farlowe and Amen Corner but eventually collapsed with huge debts. Oldham and Calder went their separate ways with Calder managing Scott Walker, Eddy Grant and even The Bay City Rollers.

Chris Chappel (1952 -   )

After leaving Trinifold where he was a management assistant Chris moved to America and became a tour manager for Bruce Springsteen and then to Canada where he took the same position with Michael Bublé. He also tour-managed for David Bowie – Glass Spider (1987), Sound + Vision (1990), and Tin Machine (1991-1992). and for Bryan Adams. He is now retired and living in Suffolk.

Trevor Churchill (1941 -   )

After graduating in 1965 with a degree in chemistry from Oxford University, Churchill managed several record labels including Bell Records, Rolling Stones Records, Tamla Motown UK and Polydor. Since 1977 he has been Business Affairs Director at Ace Records, Britain's leading reissues record company.

Bill Curbishley (1942 -   )

Curbishley began working for The Who's label, Track Records, in 1971, leaving in 1974 to establish Trinifold Management with his then-wife Jackie. Trinifold initially managed The Who and The Steve Gibbons Band and later acquired Judas Priest, Robert Plant and Jimmy Page. Curbishley was a producer of several films including *Quadrophenia*, *McVicar* (starring Roger Daltrey) and *The Railway Man* (starring Colin Firth).

Jackie Curbishley (1943 - 2016)

Jackie founded Trinifold Management with her husband but resigned her directorship in 1995 after the couple divorced. She later divided her time between homes in Spain, London and Barbados and worked as a script editor and translator. She died in London in December 2016.

Chris Curry (1946 -   )

After working for 13 years with Sinclair Radionics during which he was involved with the development of Clive Sinclair's C5 electric vehicle, and the Sinclair Executive electronic calculator, Curry left to co-found Acorn Computers with Herman Hauser and Andy Hopper. In 1983 he started Redwood Publishing with Michael Potter and Christopher Ward. One of their magazine titles was *Acorn User*. In 1985 he founded General Information Systems Ltd (GIS) to develop systems for cashless money. The company was wound up in 2023.

Eric Easton (1927 - 1995)

Easton was an old-style music business operator who'd started out playing the organ in music halls. He teamed with Andrew Oldham in 1963 to co-manage The Rolling Stones but was ousted in 1965 in favour of New Yorker Allen Klein. Easton fought the case in the courts and was awarded a substantial sum. He emigrated to Florida in 1980.

Allen Ellett (1943 -   ))

Allen Ellett came from East Ham and was the keyboard player with The Moments, for whom future Small Face Steve Marriott was the singer. Peter helped develop their mod image. Ellett went on to do sessions with The Who, Jimmy Powell and The Five Dimensions Neil Christian and The Crusaders, Jimmy James and The Vagabonds and The V.I.P.'s (later to become Spooky Tooth). The music work became an increasingly unreliable source of income, so he became an inspector for the Department of Health and Security while doing occasional local gigs as The Rockin' Baron.

John Emery (1943 -   )

John Emery trained in journalism at a sports agency in Fleet Street. In 1964 he joined Beat Publications to write for *The Beatles Book Monthly* and *Beat Instrumental*. He was then invited to join KG Publicity run by former music journalist Keith Goodwin which represented acts such as Dusty Springfield, Johnny Kidd and the Pirates, and Jimmy James and the Vagabonds. After a year on the Jimmy James account Peter Meaden asked him to work for the band full time. After two years he returned to Fleet Street to write for the *Evening Standard* and the *Daily Mail*. In 1975 Peter contacted him again to work for The Steve Gibbons Band. After Peter's death he continued to work for the *Evening Standard* as well as contributing to music publications. In 2004 he published a book of short stories, *Dream On*.

Steve Gibbons (1941 -   )

The Steve Gibbons Band continues touring but hasn't released an album since *Chasing Tales* in 2008. He also makes appearances as The Dylan Project where he performs his own material alongside songs of Bob Dylan. He lives with his wife Suzie in Edgbaston. They have two children.

Caroline Guinness (1954 -   )

After working as a receptionist at Trinifold, Caroline made rock and pop videos. In 1988 she co-founded the HIV-Aids charity Positively Women. In 1998 she met the actor Mark McGann at a party and married him in February 2000. The McCanns live in Somerset with their dog Ruby Belle. She has a daughter from a previous marriage.

Tony Hall (1928 - 2019)

Peter was dismissive of Tony Hall but few in the music business had such a wide-range of experience from compering (*Oh Boy!*) and radio presenting (Radio Luxemburg) to promoting (Decca Records) and record producing (for Decca's jazz label Tempo). Tony Hall Enterprises, started in 1967, was Britain's first independent music promotion company and worked with artists ranging from Scott Walker to Jimi Hendrix and The Who. He later managed arranger/composer Paul Buckmaster, The Real Thing and Loose Ends. Towards the end of his life, he reviewed records for *Jazzwise*.

John Michael Ingram (1931 - 2014)

Ingram opened John Michael, the first male boutique, on the King's Road in 1957 thus establishing Chelsea as a fashion centre in London and preparing the way for 'Swinging London.' His next venture, Sportique, was on Old Compton Street in Soho. He would open other shops on Bond Street and, eventually, Savile Row. His designs were stylish and innovative but never gaudy. In the late Seventies he founded Design Intelligence, one of the first British fashion forecasting agencies.

Jimmy James (1940 -   )

The Vagabonds disbanded in 1970, having been originally formed in Jamaica in 1960. James had ownership of the name so recruited a new all-white Vagabonds line up in 1973 that had UK hits with 'I'll Go Where Your Music takes Me,' 'Now is the Time' and 'Disco Fever.' Based in London since being discovered by Peter in 1965 James continues to perform in Europe, on cruise lines, and at soul or mod-themed weekenders.

Peter Jones (1930 - 2015)

As editor of *Record Mirror* from 1964 Jones helped promote The Beatles, Stones and early Motown music. Using pseudonyms, he wrote biographies of The Beatles and Stones and contributed to *The Beatles Book Monthly* as Billy Shepherd. He left *Record Mirror* in 1972 and joined *Billboard* as UK news editor and then special issues editor until his retirement in 1997.

Ronnie Jones (1937 -   )

After coming to England with the USAF Jones started a music career with the first version of Blues Incorporated with Alexis Korner, Jack Bruce, Cyril Davis, Johnny Parker and Ginger Baker. He later formed The Nightimers with guitarist John McLaughlin. After moving to Italy, where he still lives, he joined the cast of the musical *Hair* and in 1976 had a hit with 'Funky Bump'. Since moving permanently to Italy in 1979 he has worked as a musician, DJ and host on Italian TV and radio. He tours regularly with his band The Soul Syndicate.

Norman Jopling (1944 -   )

Jopling left music journalism in 1973 to work for CBS Records before moving to New York where he concentrated on song writing. In the Eighties he co-authored illustrated books on the Beatles, Cliff Richard and John Lennon. Since 1988 he has originated reissues of albums. He recounted the story of his career as a music journalist in *Shake It Up Baby!* published in 2015.

Patrick Kerr (1941 - 2009)

After making a name for himself as a choreographer and demonstrator of new dances on *Ready Steady Go!* he and his wife, Theresa Confrey, set up a boutique, Hem and Fringe, in Pimlico. In 1978, they opened a dance studio in Cambridge that developed into the Bodywork Company Dance Studio – now part of the government's prestigious Dance and Drama Awards Scheme, training future dancers and singers for West End productions.

Kenny Laguna (1948 -   )

After producing albums for The Steve Gibbons Band Laguna continued his electic career. His 2000 compliation album Laguna Tunes has tracks by Darlene Love, Tony Orlando, Bill Medley, Bow Wow Wow, and Little Roger and the Goosebumps. His most enduring musical relationship has been with Joan Jett who he has produced and managed since 1979. He was inducted with Joan Jett and the Blackhearts into the Rock and Roll Hall of Fame in 2015.

Kit Lambert (1935 - 1981)

After splitting from The Who in the mid-Seventies Lambert became increasingly dependent on alcohol. He had a home in Venice where he spent most of his time. He died in London in April 1981 of a cerebral haemorrhage after falling down a flight of stairs. Some believed the fall was caused by drink, others suggested that he'd been pushed by a coke dealer who believed he'd been wronged.

Jack Lyons (1943 -   )

After moving to London in 1960 Cork-born Jack Lyons – 'Irish Jack' – saw The Who in 1962 when they were The Detours. He introduced himself to Pete Townshend, they hit off, and he became part of The Who's family, travelling to gigs in their van, lugging gear, selling tickets and, in the process, inspiring songs like 'I Can't Explain', 'Substitute' and 'Happy Jack' and the album *Quadrophenia*. He worked for the London Electricity Board until returning home to Cork in 1968 where he became firstly a bus conductor and then a postal worker.

Caroline Maudling (1946 - 2017)

In November 1963 the *Evening Standard* refered to Maudling as "one of the best publicised teenagers in the country." The daughter of the Tory Chancellor of the Exchequer Reginald Maudling and the actress Beryl Laverick, she had enrolled at the Central School of Speech and Dama, been offered a role in the film *The Chalk Garden*, and had a *Daily Mail* column as 'The Travelling Teenager' that took her to places like Cairo, Peking and Moscow. In 1964 she hooked up with Radio Caroline's Ronan O'Rahilly and her 18th birthday party took place at 11 Downing Street with Mike d'Abo's The Band of Angels as entertainment. Her planned careers as an actress and model didn't take off and the only press mentions after 1964 were for having a child out of wedlick in Kenya (1969), marrying a businessman in Johannesburg (1969), getting divorced (1972) and identifying her brother's body after he threw himself from a tower block (1999). Her death in 2017, by which time she was living in a flat in Hatfield, went unreported in the press.

Angus McGill (1927 - 2015)

McGill started out on the *Newcastle Evening Chronicle* where his work was spotted by Charles Wintour, editor of London's *Evening Standard*, in 1957. He became a widely read columnist on the Standard renowned for spotting new trends in food, clothes, manners, and lifestyle. He was awarded an MBE in 1990. He spotted the potential of mod in 1962 and, under a pseudonym created a story about style-crazy teenagers from

Stamford Hill for *Town* magazine which featured Mark Feld, the future Marc Bolan. He wrote his final column for the *Evening Standard* in 2000, when he was 73.

Gerald Meaden (1944 - 2023)
After school Gerald went to work at Heal's in Tottenham Court Road. He married his wife Alex in 1977 and had three children, Joseph, Robert and Ruth. The family moved to Brighton and he set up his own carpeting business, Chelsea Carpets, in the fashionable Kemptown area. He later ran another two carpet businesses in Brighton.

Stanley Meaden (1906 - 1992)
In 1985 his home at 7 Cuthbert Road was subject to a compulsory purchase order due to planned roadworks. Eventually, it was spared demolition but became an end of terrace house. Stanley and Rosina moved to a Methodist nursing home in Muswell Hill where Stanley died in 1992 and Rosina in 2002.

Wendy Meaden nee Young (1945 -   )
Wendy lives and works as an artist in North London.

Andrew Loog Oldham (1944 -   )
Since the collapse of Immediate Records in 1970 Oldham has enjoyed a varied career of book writing, record producing and radio presenting – mainly in the US, Canada and Colombia. His three volume memoir *Stones*, *2Stoned* and *Stone Free* offered a fascinating glimpse into his career. For ten years he appeared daily on SiriusXM for the Underground Garage channel. Since then he has partnered with the Double Elvis network to present his *Sounds and Vision* podcast. Between writing and broadcasting he has produced artists including Charly Garcia, Argentinian band Los Ratones Paranoicos and

Canadian artist Ché Aimee Dorval. He married Colombian model Esther Farfán in 1977 with whom he has a son, Maximilian, and lives mainly in Bogota. He was treated for cocaine addiction in 2005.

Ronan O'Rahilly (1940 - 2020)

After arriving in London in 1957 O'Rahilly developed a knack for feeling the pulse of the times. He named and ran The Scene in 1963, launched the pirate ship Radio Caroline in 1964, managed Georgie Fame and Alexis Korner, formed the label Major Minor Records, executive produced *The Girl on a Motorcycle* starring Marianne Faithfull, assembled The Loving Awareness Band to spread the message of psychedelic guru Ram Dass (Richard Alpert) and even briefly managed the Detroit agitprop band MC5. He was best man at Mickey Tenner's wedding. He was diagnosed with vascular dementia in 2012 and died in Ireland in 2020.

Susie Orbach (1946 -   )

Orbach went on to become a well-known psychotherapist, psychoanalyst, writer and social critic. She is the author of *Fat is a Feminist Issue* and gained press attention when it was discovered that she was being consulted by Princess Diana in the Nineties. Orbach was briefly married to novelist Jeanette Winterson.

Sandy Roberton (1942 - 2022)

In 1968 Roberton set up September Productions to manage and produce acts like The Liverpool Scene, Steeleye Span and Plainsong. In 1977 he formed Rockburgh Records and three years later established Worlds End Management to look after the careers of producers, mixers and sound engineers. In 1985 he moved to LA where he continued to manage. He died in London from cancer.

Franc Roddam (1946 -   )

After filming *Quadrophenia* Roddam made several other movies including the Lords of Discipline, The Bride and K2 but his greatest successes have come from formatting, writing, and producing for TV. He was the format creator for the drama series *Auf Wiedersehen Pet* as well as a writer and executive producer and he came up with the concept of MasterChef which he executive produced 2005-2015. MasterChef became an international programme available in 200 countries and with many local versions.

Sandy Sarjeant (1947 -   )

Althea 'Sandy' Sarjeant came from Kensal Green and was discovered at The Scene by the *Ready Steady Go!* team who invited her to audition to become a regular dancer on the show. She later appeared as a dancer on the German TV show *Beat Club* and recorded a single 'Can't Stop the Want' for German Polydor. She married Ian McLagan of The Small Faces in 1968 but the couple divorced in 1972. She lives in West London.

Iain Sinclair (1943 -   )

Sinclair founded Iain Sinclair Design in 1964 and remains a director with his son Grant Sinclair. The company is a design house that conceives, designs, and develops highly innovative consumer products for global markets. It uses an in-house team of specialist industrial designers, electronic/mechanical engineers and CGI artists.

June Southworth (1940 - 2017)

June was one of the first writers to work on *Fabulous* magazine and, as such, a pioneer female music journalist. After *Fabulous* she spent 30 years as a feature writer for the *Daily Mail*. Before coming to London to write for the girls' weekly *Roxy* she was a librarian in her native Blackpool.

Guy Stevens (1943 - 1981)

Stevens continued to be a major influence in the British music business. He managed the Sue catalogue in the UK, brought Chuck Berry to Britain for his first post-prison tour, became head of A&R at Island Records, produced Spooky Tooth, produced the iconic album *Featuring the Human Host and the Heavy Metal Kids* by Hapshash and the Coloured Coat, introduced lyricist Keith Reid to keyboard player Gary Brooker and named the resulting band Procol Harum, served time in prison for drug offences, produced albums for Free, Heavy Jelly and Mighty Baby, conceived, named and produced albums for Mott The Hoople, and in 1979 produced *London Calling* by The Clash. He died in 1981 from an overdose of prescription drugs he was taking to cure his alcoholism.

Gina Strauss (1946 - 2004)

Gina was born in Cape Town in 1946. She came to England with her mother, brother, and sister in 1951 and later attended The King Alfred School in Golders Green. In the Sixties she became addicted to hard drugs. She married Charles Underwood in 1968, lost both her legs after falling under a train in the Seventies, divorced, and married fellow amputee, Tony Timbrell, in 1981. She died in November 2004.

Mickey Tenner (1947 -   )

Born in Stepney Tenner got his first job at the Mayfair Hotel on Stratton Street in 1961. Between 1964-1967 he was Programme Planner at Radio Caroline. He then became a DJ in Spain before returning to London and getting involved in various business exploits from property development and lighting to video tapes. In the Eighties he moved to the island of Tasmania where he still runs Rod and Fly, a company that sells fly fishing products and offers instructors and guides.

Chris Stamp (1942 - 2012)

After losing control of The Who in 1975 Stamp moved to New York where he continued a downward health spiral due to drug and alcohol abuse. In 1987 he entered he entered a drug rehabilitation programme which was so successful that he spent the rest of his life working to help other addicts and alcoholics find a cure. He qualified as a therapist and established a practice in East Hampton where he used psychodrama and counselling.

Gordon Waller (1945 - 2009)

After the demise of Peter and Gordon in 1968 Waller found it hard to find a second career. He tried landscape gardening in a small Northamptonshire village, played Pharoah in a stage version of *Joseph and the Amazing Technicolour Dreamcoat*, recorded a solo album, and became a music publisher in America. In the early Noughties he reunited with Peter Asher for a series of concerts. He died in 2009 of a cardiac arrest in Norwich, Connecticut, not far from his home in Ledyard.

Vicki Wickham (1939 -   )

Opposite: At the end of his life Peter helped to style the Steve Gibbons Band who he had originally wanted to rename The Iron Boys

After being assistant producer of *Ready Steady Go!* and fashion consultant for *The Mod's Monthly*, launched in March 1964, she moved into artist management first with Dusty Springfield and then Labelle. She was a co-writer, with Simon Napier-Bell, of Springfield's big hit 'You Don't Have to Say You Love Me'. She lives in America with soul singer Nona Hendryx, formerly of Labelle.

DEDICATION

To the first mods that I met (in 1966) in Rugby, staring out over a cup of early morning coffee at the Il Cadore: John Phillpott, Tony 'Monty' Montgomery, Andy Windsor and Don Eales. In Northampton, checking out the latest full-length green leather coats at the town's first and only male boutique: Neil Spencer and Danny Smedley. Neil went on to become the editor of *NME* in the Seventies and would publish part of my Peter Meaden interview. Danny now lives in São Paulo, Brazil

PUBLISHING HISTORY

Quotes from my Peter Meaden interview were first used in the songbook *A Decade of The Who: An Authorised History in Music, Paintings, Words and Photographs* (Fabulous Music, 1977). The weekly paper *NME* published an abridged Q&A version as The Ace Face's Forgotten Story (November 17 1979). The *NME* version was then included in the mod reader *The Sharper Word* edited by Paolo Hewitt (Helter Skelter Books, 1999) and in the NME Originals magazine *Mod* (2005). Thanks to Mark Neeter of Red Planet Books for seeing the potential in the manuscript. The content and layout is exactly as I envisaged it when I first had the idea for King Mod over 20 years ago. It's been a long hard slog getting there, but it's been worth it.

INTERVIEWS

Thanks to the following people for allowing me to quiz them in person, by email or on the 'phone: Fiona Adams, Keith Altham, Peter Anders, Philip Andronicos, Peter Asher, Cyril Blackstone, Don Black, Lionel Blake, Tony Calder, David Cartwright, Chris Chappel, Trevor Churchill, Sarah Cottle, Jackie Curbishley, Roger Daltrey, Chris Diomedous, Allen Ellett, John Emery, John Entwistle, Mick Eve, Steve Gibbons, Tony Hall, Jimmy James, Ronnie Jones, Ian Maitland, Gerald Meaden, Keith Moon, Nita Nelson, Andrew Oldham, Susie Orbach, Sandy Roberton, Franc

Roddam, Sandy Sarjeant, Michael 'Mickey' Tenner, Philip Townsend, Pete Townshend, Vicki Wickham.

ASSISTANCE

Thanks to those who supplied photos, read parts of the manuscript, or gave me contact information: Richard Barnes, Frank Bontoff, Maureen Caesar, Chris Charlesworth, Norman Jopling, Meryl Laguna, Jack Lyons, Jaime Marshall, Mel Marshall, Alex Meaden, Joseph Meaden, Ruth Meaden-Jones, Simon Plater, Clara Spencer, Chris Stamp, Peter Stanfield, John Stax, Dick Taylor, Sandra Wake, Herbie Yamaguchi. Thanks particularly to the late Gerald Meaden for working hard to keep his brother's name alive.

SOURCES

Anderson, Paul, *Mods: The New Religion*, London, Omnibus Press, 2013

Barnes, Mike, *Captain Beefheart The Biography*, London, Omnibus Press, 2011

Barnes, Richard, *Mods!*, London, Eel Pie Publishing, 1979

Berry, Chuck, *Chuck Berry: The Biography*, London, Faber & Faber, 1987

Blake, Mark, *Pretend You're in a War: The Who & The Sixties*, London, Aurum Press, 2014

Clerk, Carol, *The Saga of Hawkwind*, London, Music Sales, 2004

Cohen, Stanley, *Folk Devils & Moral Panics*, St. Albans, Paladin, 1973

Cohn, Nik, ed. Burn, Gordon, *Ball the Wall*, London, Picador, 1989

Décharné, Max, *King's Road: The Rise & Fall of the Hippest Street in the World*, London, Weidenfeld & Nicholson, 2005

Ellis, Royston, *The Big Beat Scene*, London, Four Square Books, 1961

Fletcher, Tony, *Dear Boy: The Life of Keith Moon*, London,

Omnibus Press, 1998

Gorman, Paul, *The Look: Adventures in Rock Fashion*, London, Sanctuary Publishing, 2001

Hall, Stewart and Jefferson, Tony, *Resistance Through Rituals: Youth Subcultures in Post-War Britain*, London, Hutchinson, 1976

Hamblett, Charles and Deverson, Jane, *Generation X*, Tandem Books 1964

Hebdige, Dick, *Subculture: The Meaning of Style*, London, Routledge, 1979

Herman, Gary, *The Who*, London, Studio Vista, 1971

Hewitt, Paolo, *The Sharper Word: A Mod Anthology*, London, Helter Skelter, 1999

Hunt, Chris (ed), *Mod: Interviews, Reviews & Rare Photos*, London, NME Originals 2005

Johnson, David and Dunkley, Roger, *Gear Guide*, London, Atlas Publishing, 1967

Jones, Allan (ed). *The Who*, London, Uncut Ultimate Music Guide, 2011

Jopling, Norman, *Shake It Up Baby! Notes from a Pop Music Reporter 1961-1972*, Surrey, RockHistory Ltd, 2015

Levy, Shawn, *Ready, Steady, Go!: Swinging London and the Invention of Cool*, London, Fourth Estate, 2002

MacInnes, Colin, *England, Half English*, London, MacGibbon & Kee, 1961

MacInnes, Colin, *Absolute Beginners*, London, Penguin, 1964

Marsh, Dave, *Before I Get Old: The Story of The Who*, London, Plexus, 1983

Murray, Charles Shaar, *Shots from the Hip*, London, Penguin, 1991

Neill, Andy, *Ready, Steady, Go! The Weekend Starts Here: The Definitive Story of the Show that Changed Pop TV*, Berlin, BMG, 2020

Neill, Andy, and Kent, Matt, *The Complete Chronicle of The*

Who 1958-1978, London, Virgin Books, 2007

Oldham, Andrew, *Stoned*, London, Vintage 2001

Parsons, Tony, *Limelight Blues*, London, Pan, 1983

Rawlings, Terry, *Mod: A Very British Phenomenon*, London, Omnibus Press, 2000

Savage, Jon, *Teenage: The Creation of Youth 1875-1945*, London, Pimlico, 2008

Townshend, Pete, *Who I Am*, London, HarperCollins, 2012

Tyler, Andrew, *Street Drugs*, London, Hodder & Stoughton, 1986

Weight, Richard, *Mod: A Very British Style*, London, Faber & Faber, 2013

PETER MEADEN'S JUKEBOX

These are the songs he referred to in the interview. He mentioned other artists but didn't indicate a song.

Ain't Love Good, Ain't Love Proud – Tony Clarke – Chess, 1964
I Gotta Dance to Keep from Crying – The Miracles - Motown, 1963
The Monkey Time – Major Lance – Okeh, 1963
Love Me Do – The Beatles – Parlophone, 1962
It's All Right – The Impressions – ABC, 1963
Come On – The Rolling Stones – Decca, 1962
Money - The Rolling Stones – Decca, 1964 (EP)
Daddy Rolling Stone – Derek Martin – Crackerjack, 1963
You Can't Catch Me – Chuck Berry – Chess, 1956
Zoot Suit – The High Numbers – Fontana, 1964
I am The Face – The High Numbers – Fontana, 1964
The Wanderer – Dion – Laurie, 1961
I Got Love if You Want It – Slim Harpo – Excello, 1957
It Will Stand – The Showmen – Minit, 1962
Country Fool – The Showmen – Minit, 1962
Misery – The Dynamics – Big Top, 1963

ABOUT THE AUTHOR

Steve Turner is a poet, author, and journalist. His work has appeared in *The Times, Sunday Times, Rolling Stone, Q, Mojo, NME* and many other publications. His music books include *The Man Called Cash, Beatles '66, Trouble Man: The Life and Death of Marvin Gaye, A Hard Day's Write, U2 Rattle and Hum*, and *Van Morrison: Too Late to Stop Now*. He also wrote the Jack Kerouac biography *Angelheaded Hipster*, a history of the song Amazing Grace and the story of the band that played on the Titanic.

He is currently working on *Hydrogen Jukebox*, a study of the ways in which the Beat Generation influenced rock music. He has interviewed many of the greats of the rock era from Jerry Lee Lewis, Roy Orbison and Ray Charles to Paul McCartney, John Lennon, Mick Jagger, Keith Richards, David Bowie, Syd Barrett, Bruce Springsteen, Bono and Eric Clapton.

As a teenager he was affected by what he now realises was the final wave of mod when it was popularised by magazines like *Rave* and *Fabulous* and TV programmes like *Ready Steady Go!* and ceased to be the secret of just a few He bought his first pair of Levi 501s from Lord John in Carnaby Street on December 30 1965.

He met and interviewed Peter Meaden in 1975 and wrote the text for the deluxe songbook *A Decade of The Who* (1977). He first interviewed Pete Townshend in 1971 as the newly installed features editor of the monthly music magazine *Beat Instrumental*, and later in the decade interviewed Keith Moon, John Entwistle and Roger Daltrey. He still thinks 'My Generation' is one of the greatest rock singles ever recorded and the most potent distillation of teenage angst.

He has published over ten collections of poetry, several of them for children. He lives in London.

Opposite: The author (left) with Caroline Guinness (now McGann) and Peter backstage at the Rock Garden, Covent Garden, November 5, 1976

"I believe in Nina Simone
I believe in Northern Soul
I believe in Peter Meaden
I believe in rock 'n' roll"

David Holmes (featuring Raven Violet)
'Necessary Genius' (2023)